EVERYTHING IRISH

This book will give you an opportunity to

learn about Ireland

make traditional and historical things

listen to stories about Ireland

sing Irish songs

dance with leprechauns or Irish dancers.

We invite you to experience Ireland in a fun, creative way.

An old-style Irish fireside

Everything Irish

AnnMarie O'Grady

Illustrations by Stella Kearns

THE O'BRIEN PRESS
DUBLIN

First published 1998 by The O'Brien Press Ltd.,
20 Victoria Road, Dublin 6, Ireland.
Tel: +353 1 4923333; Fax: +353 1 4922777
E-mail: books@obrien.ie
Website: www.obrien.ie
Reprinted 1998, 1999, 2001.

ISBN 0-86278-557-X

British Library Cataloguing-in-publication Data
A catalogue reference for this book is available from the British Library.

4 5 6 7 8 9 10
01 02 03 04 05 06 07 08

Typesetting, layout, design, editing: The O'Brien Press Ltd.
COVER front cover photos and *inside front* photo with money bag, *inside back* cross, dancing leprechaun: Roger Digan; back cover photos and *inside front* photos with dancing leprechaun and bodhrán, *inside back* work-in-progress: Jimmy McGuinness
Colour separations: Lithoset Ltd.
Printing: The Guernsey Press Ltd.

CONTENTS

Ireland

Ireland is a small country in Europe. It is an island, which means it is surrounded by the sea.

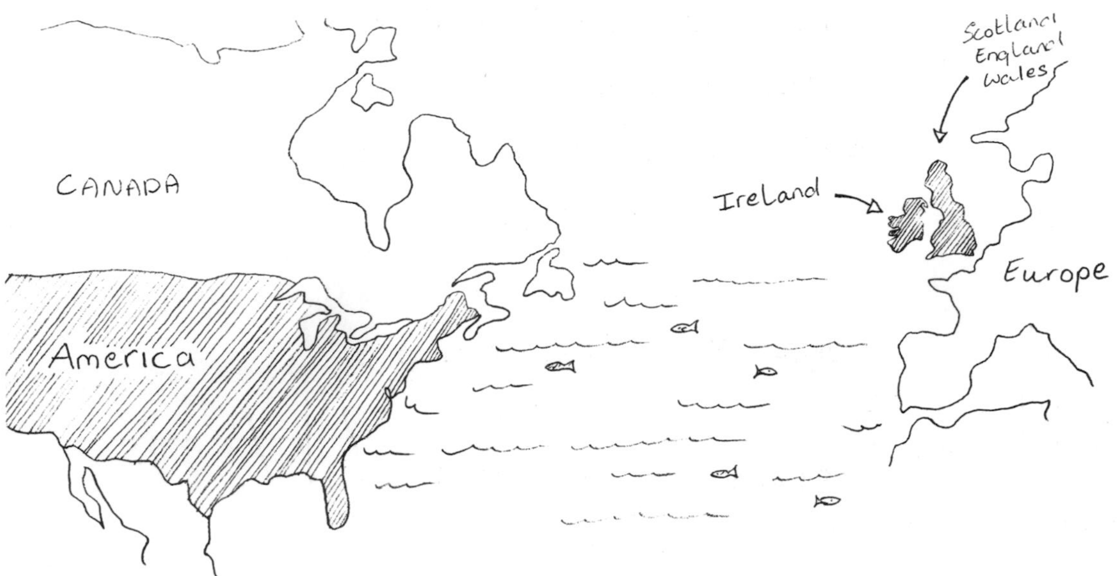

The nearest land to the WEST of Ireland is America. America is 3000 miles away.

The nearest on the EAST is Scotland. Scotland is only about 13 miles away!

RAIN

Ireland has a mild climate with a lot of rain. This makes umbrellas very popular in the winter – and sometimes in the summer too!

Many people complain about the rain. But it makes the grass very green. Maybe this is why Ireland is such a pretty country, with plenty of green fields, rivers and mountains.

BEAUTIFUL SCENERY

In Ireland there are lovely mountains, hills and valleys. There are beaches and cliffs, stony islands and green fields. People travel from all over the world – America, Canada, Australia and many other places – to see the beautiful scenery of Ireland.

Thatched Cottages

A long time ago in Ireland people used to live in very special houses. They were not big, like most houses today; they were very small and cosy. They were called thatched cottages. This is because the roof was made of straw.

The walls were painted snow white. And the roof was gold. It was sloped to let the rain run off. The cottage was only one storey high, so of course there were no stairs.

Sometimes birds made their nests in the roof! And sometimes a hen might lay her eggs there!

The most important place in the cottage was the fireplace. This was where people gathered to tell stories, sing songs or just chat about the day.

Make Your Own Thatched Cottage

YOU WILL NEED

Polyfilla • water • an empty cereal box • cardboard • paint • glue • lollipop sticks • sellotape

FOR THE ROOF

yellow felt (with sticky backing) or yellow fur

THE COTTAGE

1

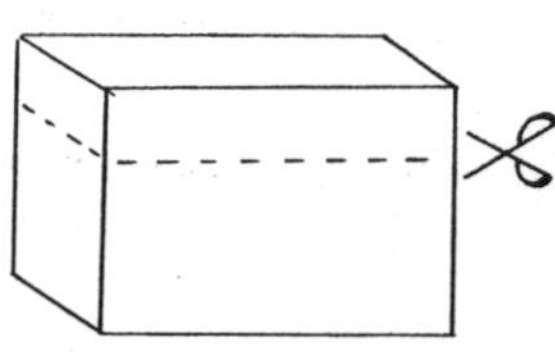

1 Cut the box to the height you want for the base of the cottage.

THE ROOF

2 Measure the length of the base of the cottage.

Cut a piece of card the same length. Fold this in two.

Sellotape this to the base (put the sellotape on the inside).

3 There will be a gap at each side of the roof in a triangle shape.

Cut some cardboard in this triangle shape. Sellotape it on, from the inside, to fill these gaps.

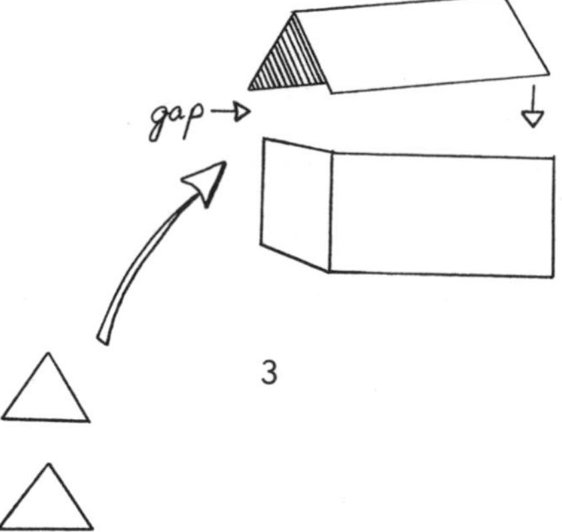

3

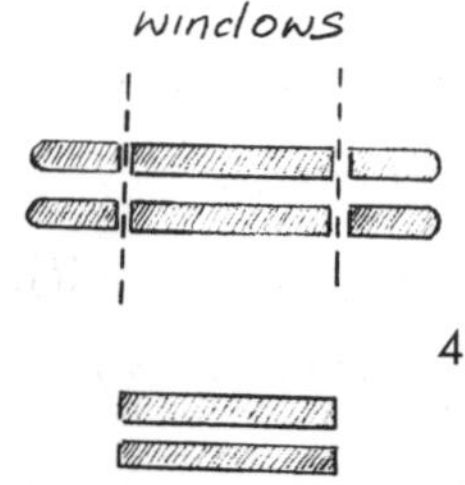

4

THE WINDOWS AND DOOR

4 Cut three lollipop sticks or pieces of cardboard to the size you want for the door. Cut four to the size you want for the windows.

Paint them whatever colour you like and allow to dry.

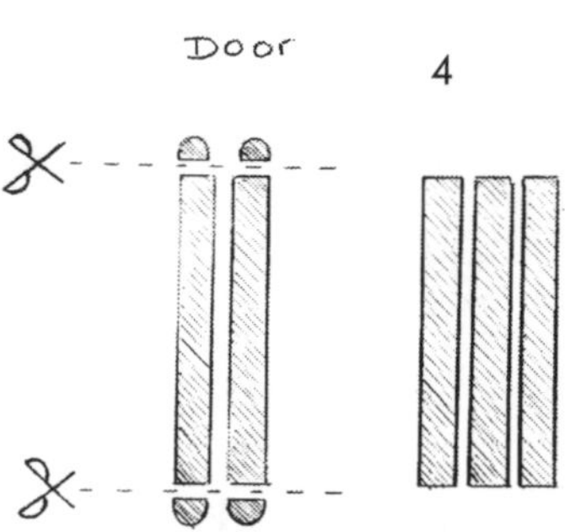

4

2

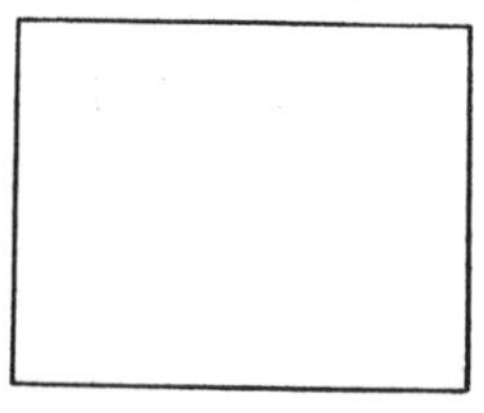

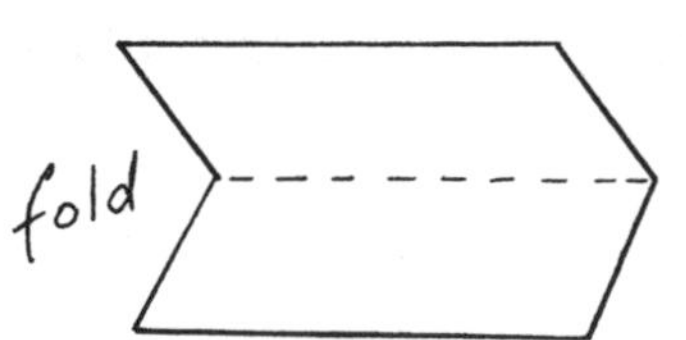

5

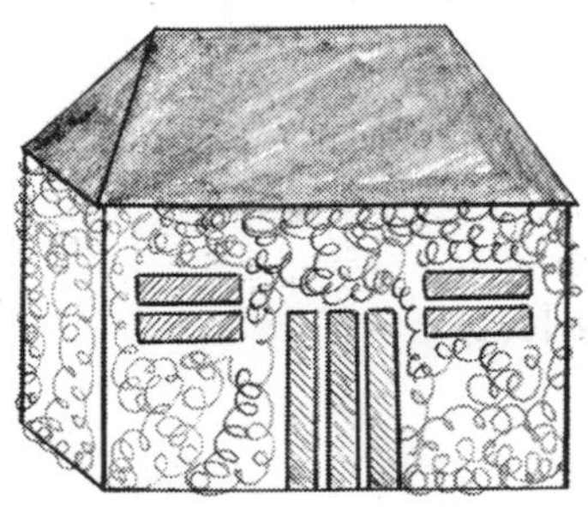

DECORATING

5 Mix the Polyfilla with water to a smooth paste. Apply this with a lollipop stick to the walls of your cottage. Stick the windows and door on while this is wet.

6 Allow to dry. When it is dry it is ready to paint. Paint the walls of the cottage white.

THATCH

You are nearly finished! All you have to do now is put on the thatch.

7 Cut the felt or fur to match the size of your roof. Now glue the yellow felt or fur to the

7

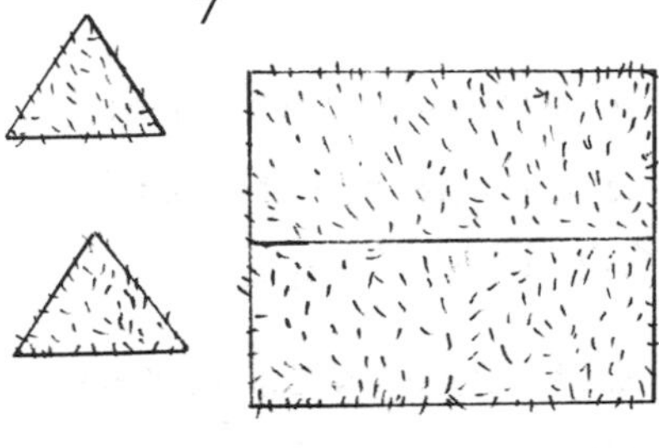

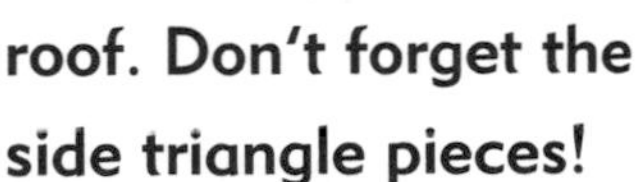

roof. Don't forget the side triangle pieces!

THE CHIMNEY

8 Cut a piece of cardboard into the shape above.

9 Now join to make into a rectangle.

10 Cut two triangles at both ends. This should slot onto the top of the house.

11 Apply Polyfilla and allow to dry.

8

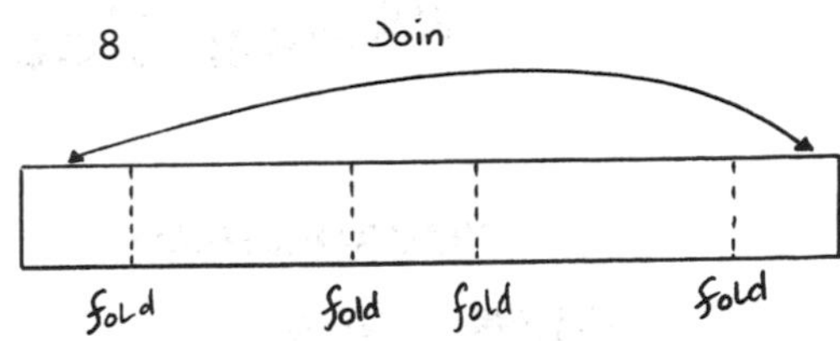

9

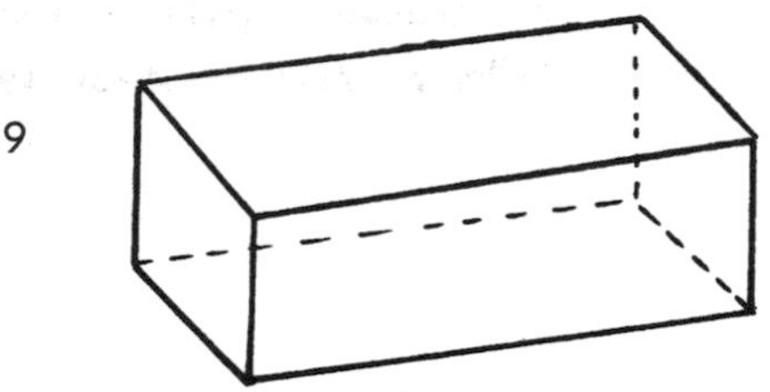

10

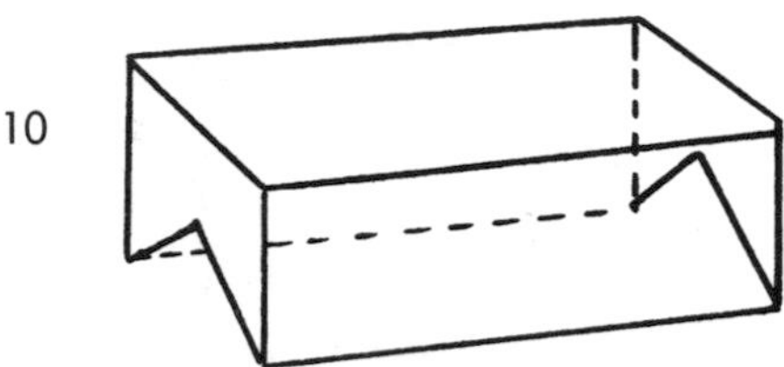

12 Paint white and put onto the roof.

Transport

A HORSE AND CART

A long time ago there were no motor cars in Ireland. People used to travel on foot or on horseback. Later, roads were made and people used a horse and cart.

They also needed to move things from one place to another. Sometimes these things were very heavy, and it was easier to pull them on the cart than to lift them. A strong horse would then pull the cart.

People in the West of Ireland also used donkeys – some still do. They put baskets on the donkey's back to carry turf home from the bog.

Make Your Own Irish Cart – just like the old days!

YOU WILL NEED

a small empty box • old newspaper • paste • 2 lollipop sticks • cardboard

• paints • scissors • sellotape • 16 small sticks • one long thin stick, the width of the empty box • 'Badge Fun' mix (see p. 25).

THE CART

1 Cut off one side of the box.

1

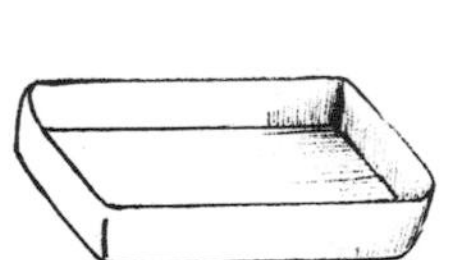

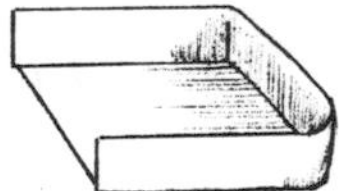

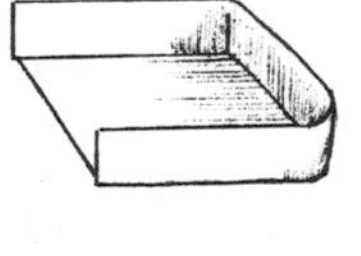

2 Glue the lollipop sticks at the top of the box. Allow to dry.

2

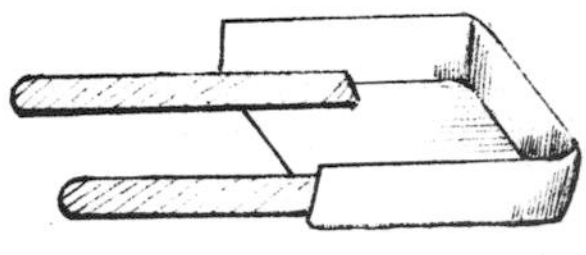

3 Tear the newspaper into small pieces. Dip into the paste and stick on all over the box. Allow to dry.

3

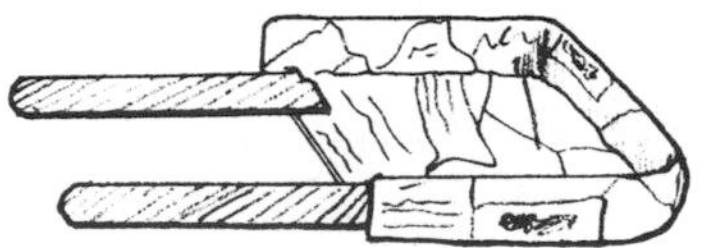

4 Paint the box and sticks brown.

THE WHEELS

5 With the 'Badge Fun' mix (p. 25), make a lump of dough the size of the circle below, and put a hole right through the centre.

5

lump of dough this size

6 Put 8 sticks (equal length) around the lump.

6

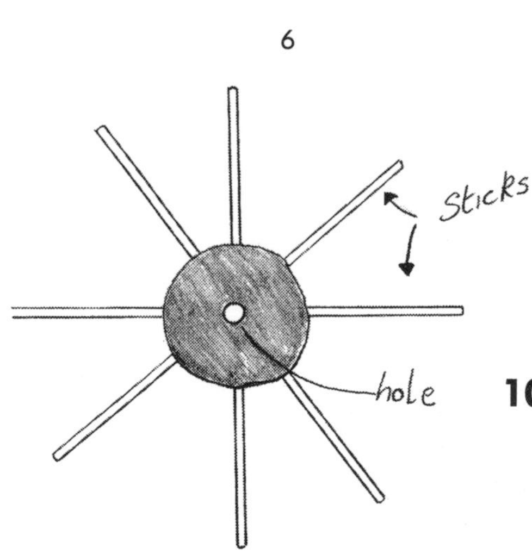

7 Roll out a dough snake and put it all around the wheel.

7

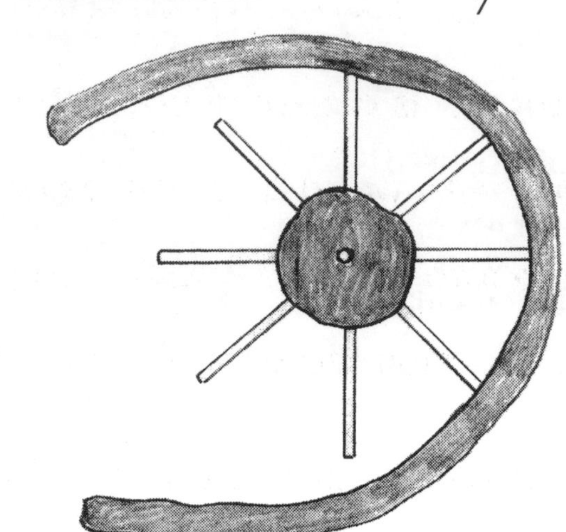

8 Now make another wheel the very same way!

9 Put them on a baking tray and leave in the oven overnight at the lowest heat. Paint the wheel black and the centre and sticks red.

PAINT

10 Put the long thin stick through the holes in both wheels. Fix on with a piece of pipecleaner.

11 Stick this onto the bottom of the cart with sellotape and cover it with brown felt or paper.

10

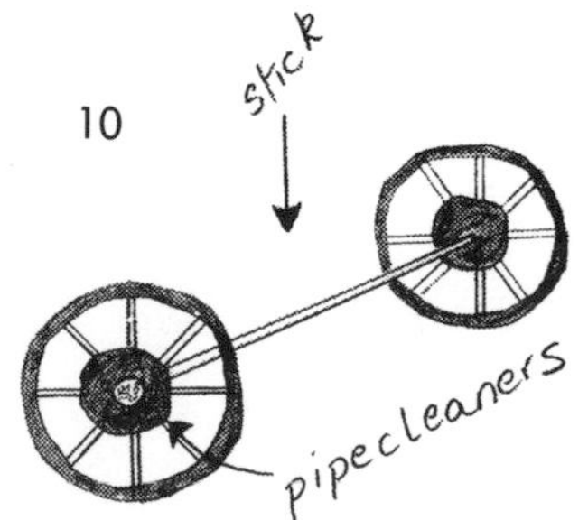

The Currach

A currach is a special boat used in the West of Ireland. It is made with wood and canvas or dried skins. The wood is made into a frame and the canvas or skins are put over this. It is painted with black tar to keep out the water.

These black boats are very light. They are driven with oars. When they are not at sea, they are turned upside down on the beach – then all the water runs out of them and they dry out.

Make Your Own Irish Currach

YOU WILL NEED

a plastic bottle • *papier maché* (mixed torn newspaper and paste) • a lollipop stick for each seat • eight sticks for oars • sticky brown paper (that looks like wood)

THE BOAT

1 Get an adult to cut the bottle into this shape:

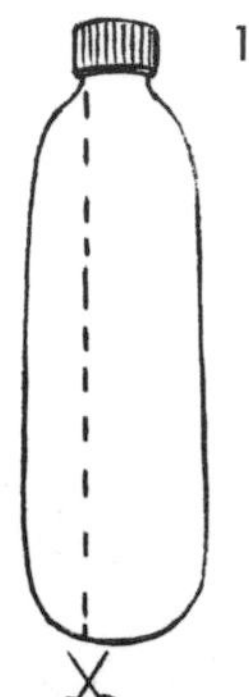
1

2 Put *papier maché* all over the bottle, inside and outside, and allow to dry. Do this twice to get a nice finish.

2

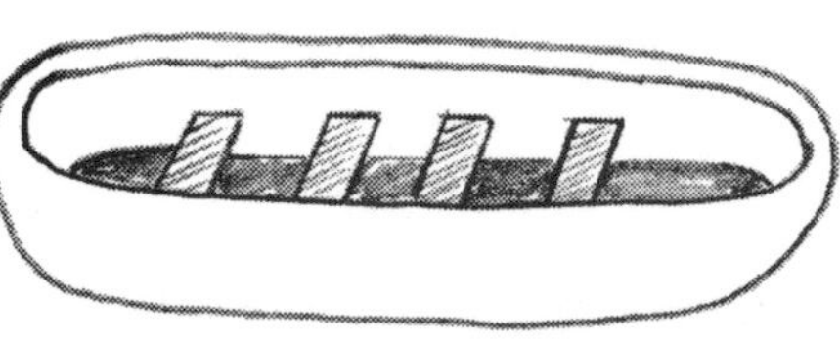
3

3 Put lollipop sticks across it for the seats. Cut to length if you need to.

4 Paint the boat black and the seats brown.

OARS

5 Cut the sticky brown paper into long strips.

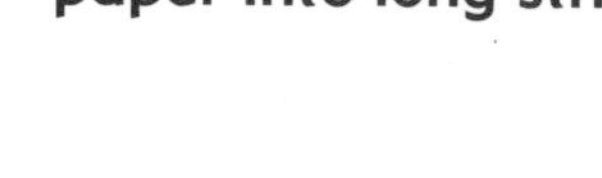

6 Fold over the sticks.

6

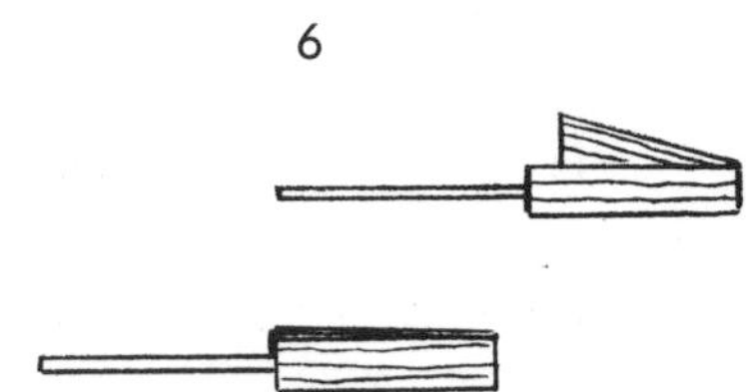

Make two for each seat.

Legends

A Story to Tell: The Children of Lir

A long, long time ago in Ireland there lived a king named Lir. Lir had a wife called Eve, and four children: Fionnuala, the eldest girl, Aed, the oldest boy, and the younger twins Conn and Fiacra. They all lived happily in a big fort on the top of a hill. Sadly, soon after the birth of the twins, Eve became ill and died. Lir and his children were very lonely, and sadness and grief filled their hearts.

Lir decided to re-marry, and his new wife was called Aoife. Aoife loved Lir and his children, and they all had happy times together. But after some time Aoife grew angry because she thought that Lir was spending too much time with his children, and that he did not love her. She became bitter, and jealous of them. 'Lir loves his children more than he loves me,' she would secretly groan to herself. She longed to get rid of the children and soon her bitterness grew into hatred.

One day she thought of a wicked, evil plan. It was a warm summer's day and Aoife took the children to a lake near their home. The children were always playful and they loved the water. But suddenly Aoife took a druid's wand from beneath her cloak and waved it at the children while she cast an evil spell on them.

The children looked at each other in horror. They were no longer children! Instead, they floated in the water in the form of four white swans.

'What evil have you done us?' Fionnuala cried out in horror.

'Ha! You are swans now, and I will have the king to myself!' said Aoife with an evil grin. 'You must spend three hundred years here in Lough Derravaragh, three hundred years on the Sea of Moyle, and three hundred years on Inish Glora. The sound of the Christian bell will announce the end of your exile.'

'Oh please,' cried the children, 'make us children again. We have done you no harm.'

When Aoife heard the children's cries she was filled with remorse. She told them that the spell was too powerful to undo – but that even though they had the appearance of swans they would be able to talk and would be blessed with the gift of singing that would comfort them over the years. Then in a state of panic she ran back to the king to tell him that the children had drowned.

The king rushed to the lakeside but he could see no sign of his children – only four white swans. Suddenly he heard Fionnuala's voice. 'Father, it is us, your children.' Fionnuala told her father the sad story of Aoife's jealousy and of the nine-hundred-year spell she had put on them. Lir was overcome with grief.

'But we have the gift of singing,' said Fionnuala. 'That will comfort you.'

Then the children sang to their father to ease his pain. Soon Lir was lost in the sound of the sweetest music he had ever heard.

He decided to leave his home and live by the lakeside. But first he punished Aoife – with a spell, he turned her into a demon of the air, banished forever to the skies.

The king visited his children every day. He told them stories and they sang to him. He loved them more than ever. He stayed with the children until he died beside the lake.

The years passed and people came from all over the world to hear the beautiful music of the swan-children.

After the three hundred years on Lough Derravaragh the children flew to the Sea of Moyle. The water was very cold and there were many wild storms. The children were afraid they might not survive. They huddled up together and wept. The time came at last for their final journey.

They flew to the waters of Inish Glora. Here it was not as cold and they knew that their time was coming to an end. This brought them hope.

A kind holy man came to spend time with them. They answered his morning chants with their sweet music and found peace on Inish Glora. One morning he came to them to tell them that a new religion of love had swept across the country. He told them about Saint Patrick and the Christian faith.

Then they heard the Christian bell and they knew their time in exile was over. The monk blessed them and their white feathers disappeared. They had their human shape back. But now they were old, nine hundred years old. They died peacefully, and the holy man buried them together in one grave.

That night he looked up to the sky and prayed for them. Then he saw five stars shining brightly in the dark. He knew that the children of Lir and their father were together in a special place.

Make Your Own Children of Lir Fridge Magnets

See Badge Fun page 25 for instructions.

the children of Lir

Saint Patrick

Ireland's patron saint is Saint Patrick. His feast day is 17 March.

On this day parades, singing and dancing can be seen in many countries throughout the world, such as America and Australia. These countries have big Irish communities – which means that many Irish people went to live there.

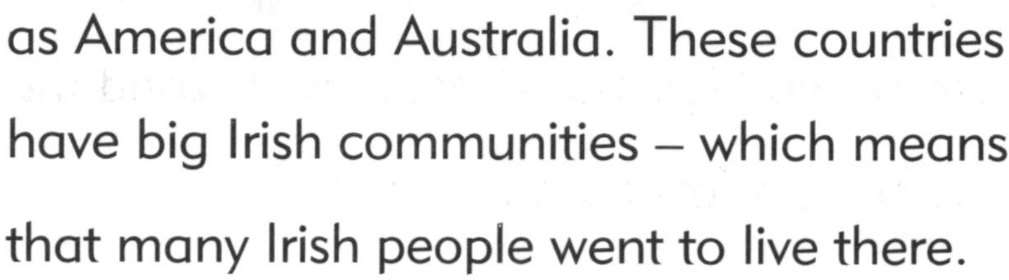

Saint Patrick brought the Christian faith to Ireland and explained the Holy Trinity with a shamrock. This is why people wear the shamrock on his special day. The shamrock is now Ireland's national flower.

Stories say that Saint Patrick banished all the snakes out of Ireland!

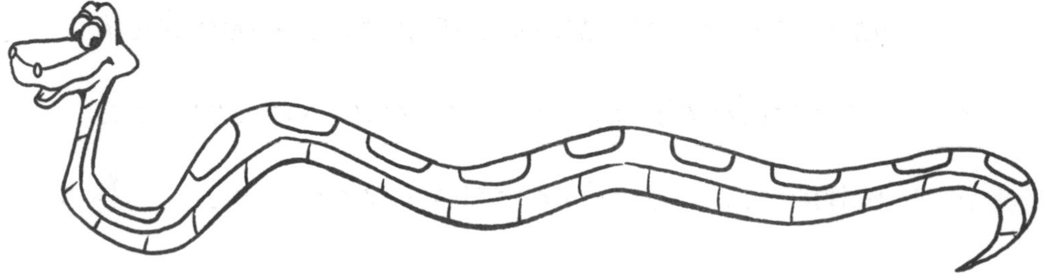

A STORY TO TELL ...

The Story of Saint Patrick

Saint Patrick was born a long, long time ago in Roman Britain. When he was only sixteen years old he was captured by pirates. He was brought to Ireland as a slave. Poor Patrick was left to herd cattle and sheep on the rainy, cold hills of Ireland. Patrick was lonely far away from home. Sometimes he was so hungry he would eat the food left for the pigs and sheep. He learned the Irish language but he had few friends to talk to.

Patrick was always thinking of ways to escape his lonely life in Ireland. He was very brave and decided he would run away. He made a long and dangerous journey to the seaside where he got on a ship. It took him days to travel the seas but soon he reached Britain, and he made his way home. His parents were thrilled to see their son again after so many years. They hugged and cried and laughed together. The time the spent together was very special.

But one night Patrick had a strange dream. In the dre he heard a message which told him to return to Irelan He heard a voice which said he must help the Irish pe with their religion. So Patrick first went to France to become a priest. He then made his way back to the l where he had once been a lonely slave.

Patrick was a fearless leader. He spoke the Irish lang which he had learnt as a boy. He picked a shamrock the ground – the shamrock has three leaves and Patr used them to describe God the Father, God the Son God the Holy Spirit. Soon the people started to listen Patrick's teaching. He converted so many and sprea message so far across the land that he is now the pa saint.

A STORY TO TELL …

The Story of Saint Patrick

Saint Patrick was born a long, long time ago in Roman Britain. When he was only sixteen years old he was captured by pirates. He was brought to Ireland as a slave. Poor Patrick was left to herd cattle and sheep on the rainy, cold hills of Ireland. Patrick was lonely far away from home. Sometimes he was so hungry he would eat the food left for the pigs and sheep. He learned the Irish language but he had few friends to talk to.

Patrick was always thinking of ways to escape his lonely life in Ireland. He was very brave and decided he would run away. He made a long and dangerous journey to the seaside where he got on a ship. It took him days to travel the seas but soon he reached Britain, and he made his way home. His parents were thrilled to see their son again after so many years. They hugged and cried and laughed together. The time they spent together was very special.

But one night Patrick had a strange dream. In the dream he heard a message which told him to return to Ireland. He heard a voice which said he must help the Irish people with their religion. So Patrick first went to France to become a priest. He then made his way back to the land where he had once been a lonely slave.

Patrick was a fearless leader. He spoke the Irish language which he had learnt as a boy. He picked a shamrock from the ground – the shamrock has three leaves and Patrick used them to describe God the Father, God the Son and God the Holy Spirit. Soon the people started to listen to Patrick's teaching. He converted so many and spread his message so far across the land that he is now the patron saint.

Badge Fun and Fridge Magnets

You may like to make badges for your friends and family for Saint Patrick's Day, or for other special Irish days. Or, you may like to make fridge magnets which will remind you of what you have learned in this book. Badges and magnets are lots of fun and easy to make.

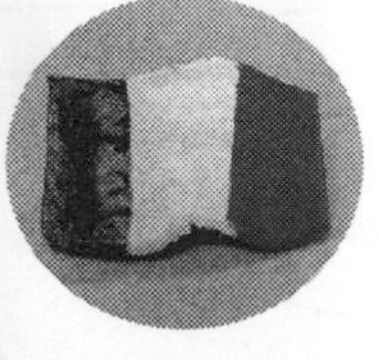

YOU WILL NEED

100g plain flour • 50g salt • 80ml water • 1 teaspoon cooking oil • glue • badge pins or packs of backs for badges or magnets (you can get these in craft shops) • quick-dry varnish (get in craft shops)

1

Mix salt, flour and cooking oil in a bowl. Add the water a little at a time until you have a smooth paste.

2 Shake a little flour onto a worktop and roll the dough out on it (like pastry). Don't make it too thin or it will break.

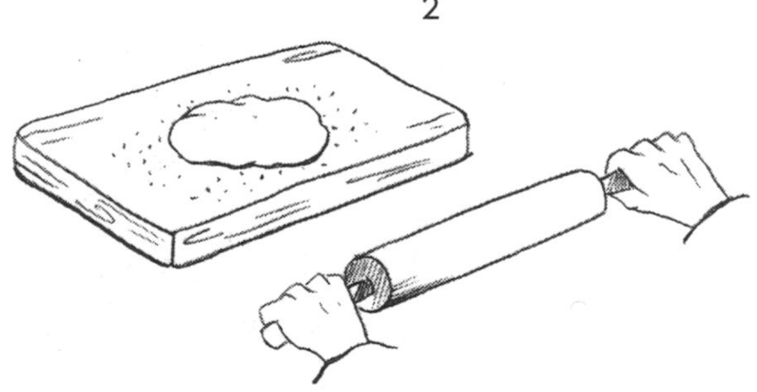

Your dough is ready to use!

3 Here are some shapes to give you ideas. Trace onto paper, cut out, then mark around the shape on your dough with a stick or pencil. Cut out with the stick.

4 When the shapes are ready put them in the oven and leave at the lowest setting overnight.

5 Allow to cool, then paint the shapes in different colours.

6 You must varnish them for a good finish and to make them last longer.

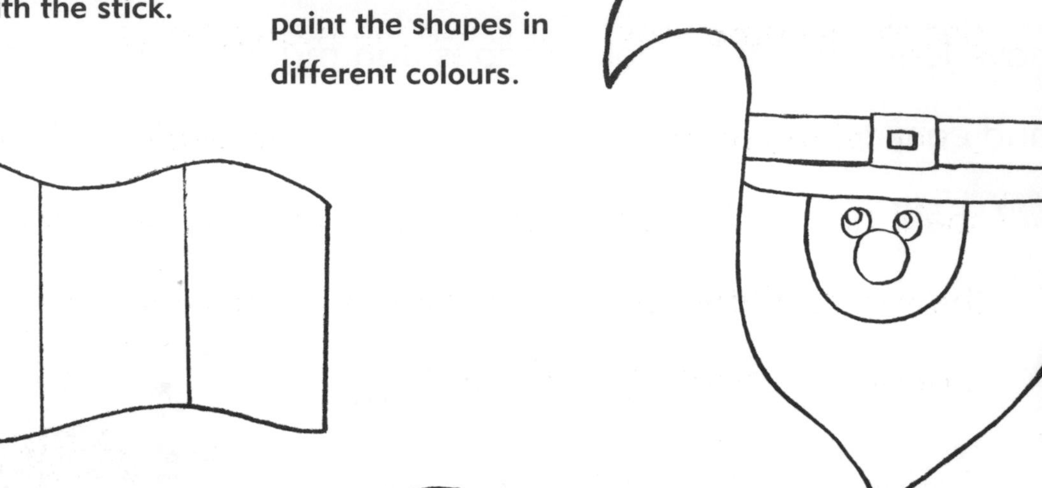

the Irish flag

Leprechaun

Celtic Cross

Why not make up your own Irish shapes?

Shamr

The Book of Kells

After Saint Patrick died people began to follow his message. They started to enjoy prayer and learning. Some people became monks and lived in monasteries.

Some of the monks spent their whole life writing. They spent hours with beautiful colours, drawing and re-writing the words of the gospel. They made some of the most magnificent books in the world.

One of these is called the Book of Kells. It can be seen in Dublin, in a college called Trinity College. It was all written by hand, so this is the only copy of the book in the whole world.

There are a lot of spirals and unusual designs throughout the book, and lots of beautiful colours.

The dog in the illustration here is from the Book of Kells.

The alphabet in Irish manuscript lettering is a little different from the English alphabet you know. There are eight letters missing!

Write Your Name the Celtic Way

Now have a go at writing your own name in this Irish script. Just go to each letter and you will see the manuscript lettering above it.

a b c d e f

g h i l m n

o p r s t u

Remember you will not be able to write your name if any of the following letters are in it:

J K Q V W X Y Z

But you can make up letters like the Irish ones, as we did! Have a go ...

the missing letters

j k q v w x y z

When you've written your name why not put some spirals around it to make it look pretty!

Irish Treasures

HIGH CROSSES

The Celtic cross at Clonmacnois

There are many high crosses in Ireland. They can be seen all over the country. They were made by monks over a thousand years ago. They are made of stone.

The monks wanted to teach people the Bible stories, so the crosses tell these stories in pictures.

They also wanted their crosses to look beautiful. The crosses have lots of designs carved in the stone.

These crosses have a ring in the top part where the two arms meet. They are often called Celtic crosses.

If you would like to make a high cross of your own then go to Badge Fun on page 25.

CHALICES

The monks also made beautiful chalices. They were made of gold and silver, with precious stones and coloured glass set into lovely patterns.

Sometimes these chalices were lost or hidden, because the monasteries were attacked. They often lay hidden for hundreds of years. The Derrynaflan Chalice was found in 1980 – it had been lying hidden in a bog for over a thousand years.

The Derrynaflan Chalice – you can see it in the National Museum in Dublin.

The Ardagh Chalice – also in the National Museum.

THE ARDAGH CHALICE

The most famous chalice is the Ardagh Chalice. This was used to give out wine in the church. It is made from silver and gold. It is decorated with shapes and spirals and large, coloured studs.

The Tara Brooch

THE TARA BROOCH

Tara was the place where the most powerful kings of ancient Ireland lived. This brooch is a special Irish brooch, and was used to tie on the cloaks that men and women wore long ago. This also has pretty designs and colours.

Saint Brendan

Did you know that this man *may* have sailed to America a thousand years before Christopher Columbus? We will never know, but it is possible.

Saint Brendan was an Irish monk. He was born in Kerry just after Saint Patrick died. Brendan was a special monk. He loved adventure and, most of all, he loved to travel. He wrote about his journeys in a book.

Brendan's boat was like the currach you read about earlier. It was made from skins stretched over a wooden frame. But it had a kind of hood for shelter. It was a small boat with only a few people on board. It is very exciting to think that such a small boat could reach America. Some people find it impossible to believe. Remember, America is 3000 miles away from Ireland. That's a long trip for a little boat!

But not long ago, in 1977, a man called Tim Severin sailed to America in a boat exactly like Saint Brendan's. This proved that it was possible to do this long trip in such a small boat.

Make Your Own St Brendan Boat

YOU WILL NEED

FOR THE BOAT
see p. 16 but leave out the sticks for the seats

FOR THE HOOD AND SAILS
coloured card or paper • a single-hole punch • small thin sticks • sellotape • glue • scissors • Polyfilla or sticky playdough

THE BOAT

Make the boat just like the currach on page 16 (without the seats).

THE SHELTER

1 **Cut out a rectangle of cardboard.**

2 **Paint the same colour as the boat.**

3 **Bend over into a loop and stick onto the boat, putting the sellotape on the inside.**

1

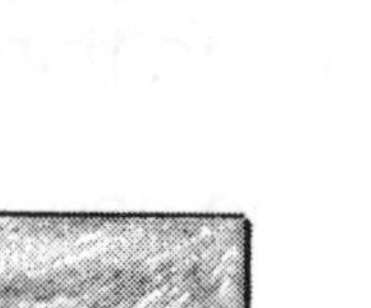

3

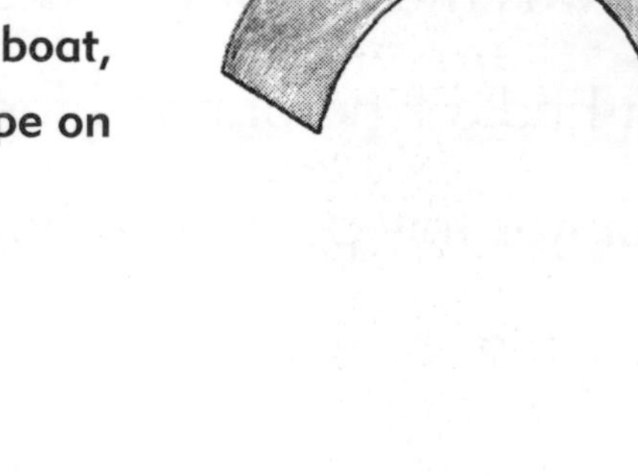

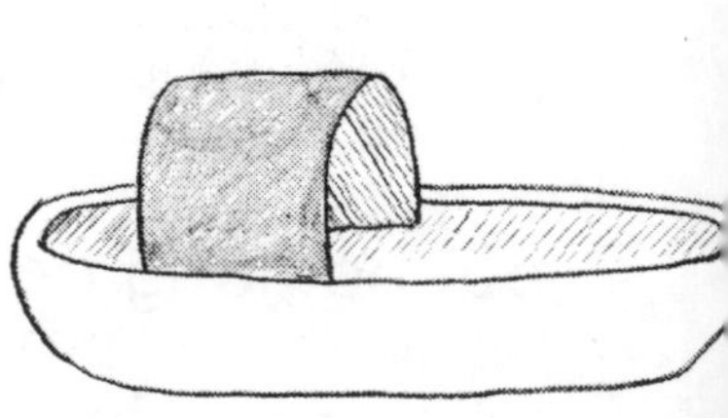

THE SAILS

Use two different-coloured pieces of card or paper, one smaller than the other. Copy or trace the high cross below onto both.

Use a single-hole punch to put a hole at the top and the bottom of the pieces of card/paper.

3 Put a thin stick through the holes. Secure with sellotape at back.

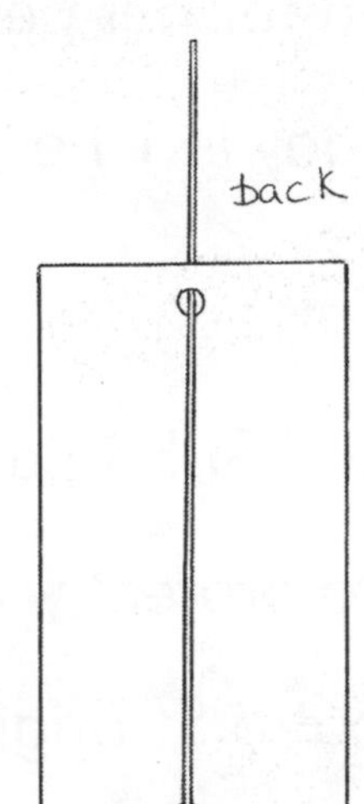

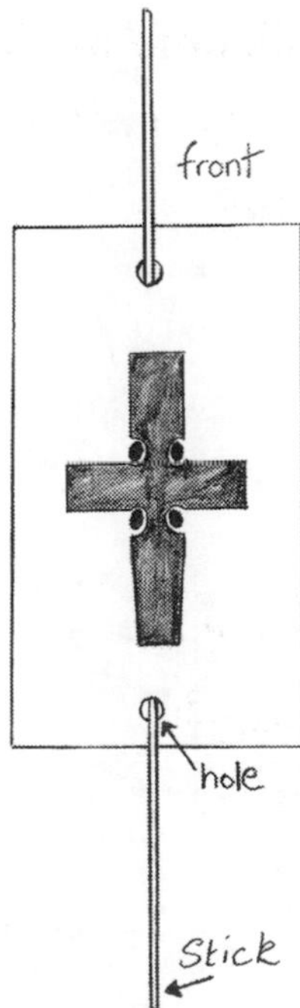

4 In the bottom of the boat put two lumps of playdough or Polyfilla. Put the two pieces of stick into the lumps so they stand steady and upright. You might paint the playdough/ Polyfilla to match the colour of the boat.

Saint Brigid

Saint Brigid is remembered for her generous nature and her kindness. Her special day is 1 February, the first day of spring.

There is a lovely cross called St Brigid's cross and it is special because it is said to protect your home from evil. Long ago people always put a St Brigid's cross over the door in their cottage. The cross is woven from rushes, which grow in boggy places. They bend easily and don't break. You can make your own Saint Brigid's cross and hang it over the door.

Make Your Own St Brigid's Cross

Here we make the Brigid's cross out of colourful pipecleaners as rushes would be impossible for many people to find. But if you can get them, do use them!

YOU WILL NEED

- **coloured pipecleaners**

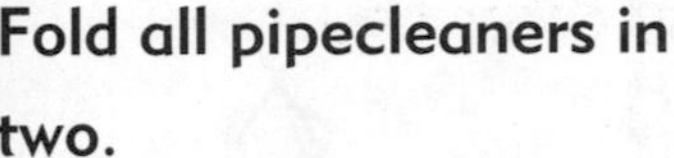

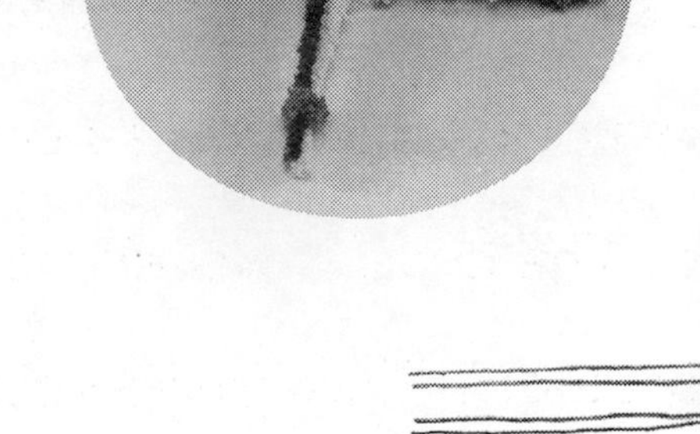

Fold all pipecleaners in two.

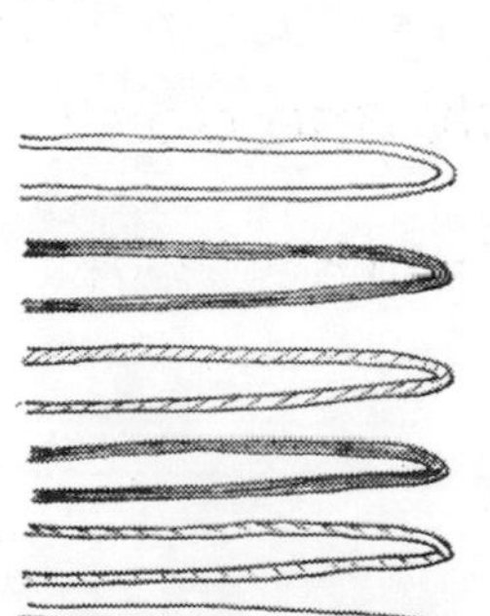

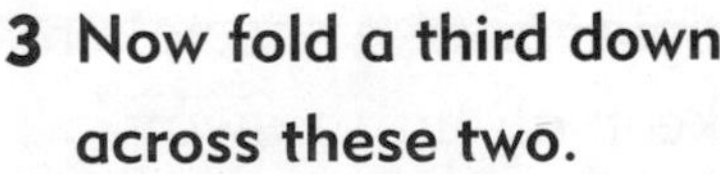

Take two of them and slot one through the other.

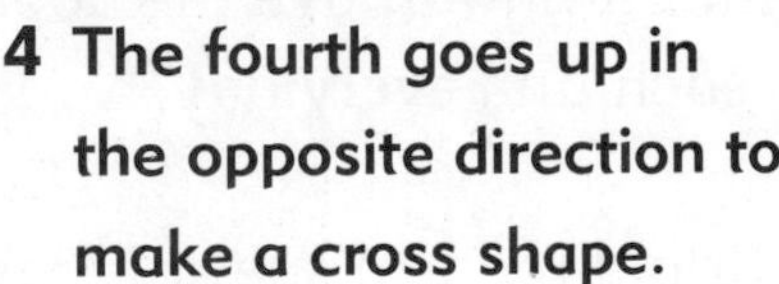

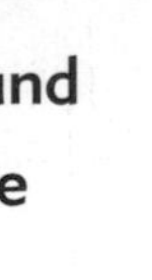

3 Now fold a third down across these two.

4 The fourth goes up in the opposite direction to make a cross shape.

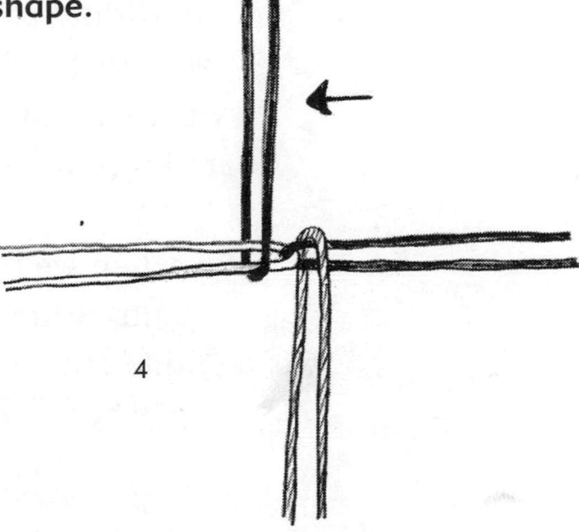

5 **Each pipecleaner after that goes over the last one used.**

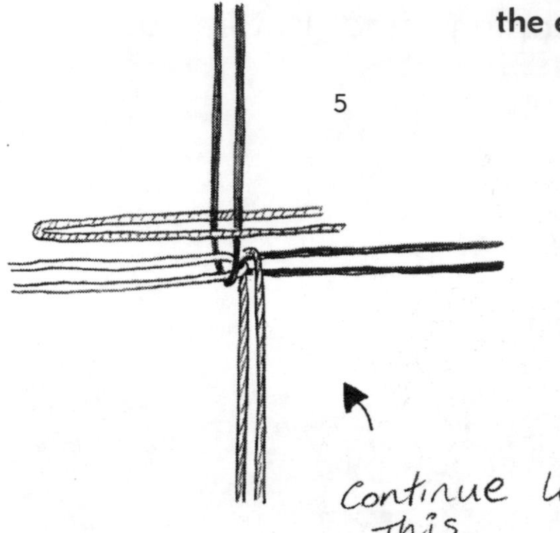

6 **Make the cross as big as you want. Then tie the ends with pieces of pipecleaner, and trim the ends.**

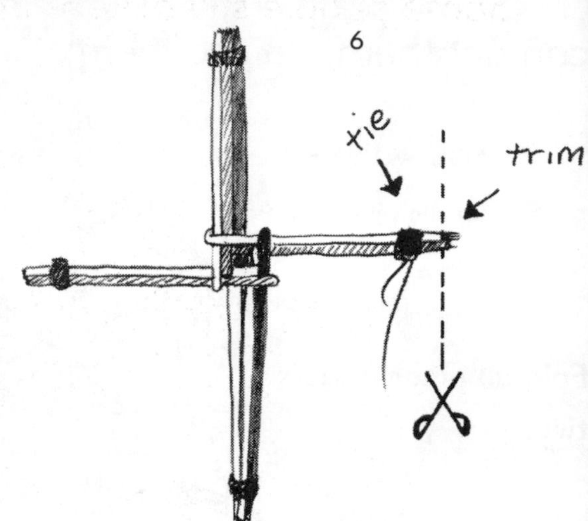

A Little Brigid Poem

Saint Brigid made a special cross
to keep all harm away,
we place it now above the door
each and every day.

Saint Brigid made a special cross
with rushes from the ground,
we use it now in all our homes
to keep them safe and sound.

So, when we're feeling troubled,
Saint Brigid's cross is here,
we've made our own with colours bright –
we have no need to fear.

The Fairies

In olden times people believed that fairies lived in Ireland. Some people still believe in them.

The fairies were said to live in thorn trees or in fairy forts. It was, and still is, very unlucky to harm the home of a fairy, and nobody would ever cut down a thorn tree. We can still see lots of them standing alone in fields in the Irish countryside today. So if you are visiting Ireland be careful not to damage any!

Fairies were known for their beautiful music. They also loved dancing and playing games.

A STORY IN VERSE ...

Maura and Her Fairy Friend

A long time ago in Ireland
when fairies lived with us,
there was a lady small and bright
who never made a fuss.

Her name was Maura of the clouds
because she dreamt and dreamt ...
... and went about her business
and 'twas no harm she meant.

The people used to laugh at her,
this lady in a dream,
but Maura always smiled at them
and never thought them mean.

One day as Maura swept her house
a fairy bright and real
came up to her and gently asked
to share a bowl of meal.

Maura fed the little dear, of course,
she really didn't mind,
and then the fairy promised her
a gift for being so kind.

Maura smiled as she was leaving,
said a farewell warm and true,
and never thought to ask her friend
for the gift that she was due.

She just went about her business
in her usual way,
and stepped outside to get her food
from the barrel the next day.

It had been almost empty
when she'd last looked inside,
but this time when she got to it
she opened her eyes wide.

Her barrel was now full of food
up to the very end,
and when she looked upon her gift
she thought of her fairy friend.

Now when a friend is hungry
or cold or feeling blue,
share the little you may have
and make their dream come true!

The Leprechaun

The leprechaun is a tiny shoemaker, known in the stories for his mischievous nature. He has a pot of gold which he keeps buried in the ground. He hides it at the end of the rainbow!

The leprechaun is dressed in green so it is very hard to spot him in the green grass. It also makes him very hard to catch. But if you are lucky enough to catch one, be careful! Leprechauns can never be trusted. They always try to get away before you find out where their pot of gold is hidden. And they play all kinds of tricks to catch you out.

Now, you can make your own laughing leprechaun, or learn to sing a leprechaun song. Or, if you'd prefer, you can just sit back and enjoy the leprechaun story.

A STORY TO TELL

Larry, the Lonely Leprechaun

Once upon a time there lived a leprechaun called Larry. He looked like all the other leprechauns in his little green suit and hat. He made and mended shoes like all the other leprechauns too.

But there was one small difference between Larry and the other leprechauns – he was lonely and he wanted a friend.

The other leprechauns didn't understand this. 'We are solitary creatures,' they would say, 'we are meant to be alone.' But Larry still felt sad and he still wanted someone to talk to.

One day as Larry was mending a fairy's shoe, he heard the sound of a little girl crying. He felt so sad that he wanted to talk to her to try and make her happy.

He left his job and went to look. Sure enough, under the tree he saw a most beautiful girl, sobbing.

'Why are you crying?' asked Larry.

The little girl didn't answer. She just cried and cried. She didn't hear anything.

'Hello, little girl,' said Larry, although she seemed big to Larry who was only tiny. 'What has you so sad on this fine day?' But he got no response, only the sad tune of her tears. Larry's heart grew sadder and lonelier. He knew that the little girl couldn't see or hear him. He went back to mending the fairy's shoe, wondering what could be wrong with such a pretty girl.

The next day Larry heard the sobbing again. He returned to the tree where he saw the little girl, crying and crying. He thought she was so beautiful that she must be a princess.

'Hello, princess. Have you lost your prince?' Larry asked. But still he got no response, only the sound of the girl's tears.

He decided to follow her home to see what was wrong. To his surprise, the little girl didn't live in a palace as a princess would. She lived in a small cottage. It looked like it might fall over if there was a storm. He stayed and watched her do her homework and help in the little cottage.

That night Larry decided he must talk to the little girl. If he did, he would be the happiest leprechaun that ever lived. And maybe he could make her happy too. But alas, there seemed to be no hope. She could not see him or hear his voice.

The next day Larry followed the little girl to school. To his surprise she worked and played all alone. The other children teased her.

'Look at your dirty shoes, they even have holes in them,' said one of the girls.

Larry couldn't believe his ears. He ran away and set to work. He got all the leftovers from all the fairy shoes he had ever made and designed the most beautiful pair of shoes you have ever seen. It took him days to finish them because he took so much care making them. They were the largest shoes he had ever made. Then, at last, they were finished.

He dragged the shoes to the tree and waited for the little girl to come. She finally arrived, and went to sit under the tree. Then she noticed the shoes. She tried them on.

'It's a miracle!' she said. 'A beautiful new pair of shoes!'

She danced and giggled with joy. 'But are they for me?' she wondered out loud.

'Oh yes,' said Larry, even though he knew she couldn't hear him. 'They are to bring you good luck.'

'Who said that?' said the little girl.

Larry couldn't speak with the shock. She had heard him speak!

'Who said that?' she asked again.

'Emmm, errrr – I-I-I did,' stuttered Larry.

And the little girl turned around and saw him. 'Hello, who are you?'

'I, errrrrr, I'm Larry,' he said nervously. 'What is your name?'

'I'm Sally. Are these shoes really for me?' she asked.

'Yes, they're a gift I made for you. I hope you like them,' said Larry with a smile.

'They are the nicest shoes I have ever seen!' she said. 'Thank you. No-one has ever made me a gift before.'

Larry felt so proud. He knew that he had really made her feel special – but he too had received a very special gift.

'But you have given me a gift, a special gift indeed,' Larry announced with a grin.

Sally looked at him in great wonder. She had brought him no gift that she could think of. 'What do you mean?' she asked.

'Up to this day no human has ever spoken to me. Today I feel special talking to you,' Larry smiled.

Sally said that it was Larry's own kindness that helped her to see him. Up to that day she had always felt too sad.

Sally and Larry talked and laughed and danced and sang for hours. It was as if they had been friends for a long time. They had never felt so happy. When they parted they knew they would see each other again. From that day forward they were very special friends.

The Laughing Leprechaun

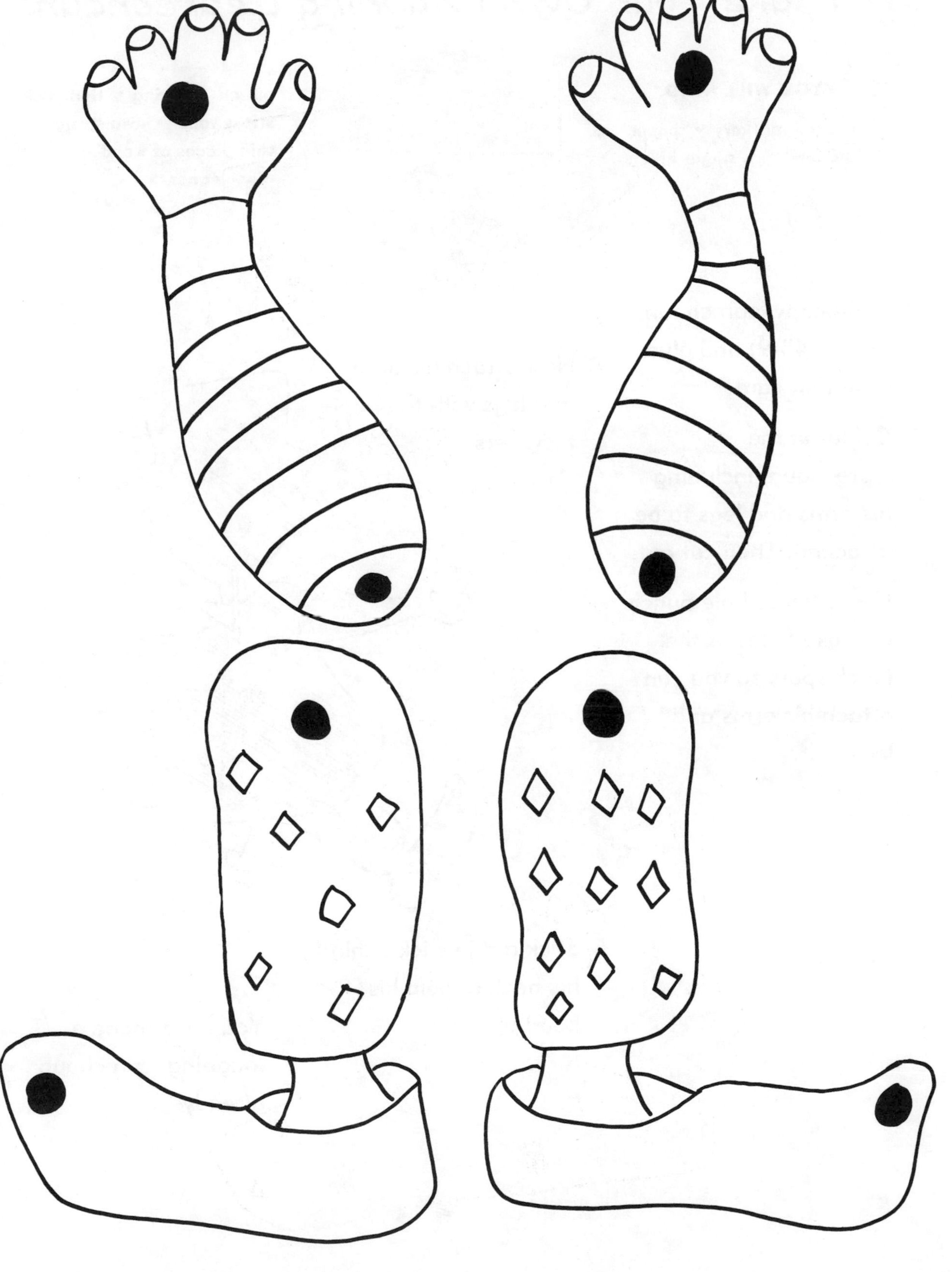

Make Your Own Laughing Leprechaun

YOU WILL NEED

coloured markers • paper fasteners • a single-hole punch • string • thin stick • sticky tape • two straight thin pieces of wood • pipecleaner

1 Photocopy leprechaun (pages 48-9) and glue onto thin card.

2 Colour in the leprechaun, including his arms and legs to be attached. Then cut out.

3 Use a single-hole punch to make holes at the black spots so you can attach his arms and legs.

4 Now attach his arms and legs with the paper fasteners.

5 Stick a thin stick behind his neck to hold his head up.

You have made a laughing leprechaun already!

Leprechaun on a String

If you would like your leprechaun to hang from a string like a puppet then continue with the following instructions ...

1 Tie two pieces of wood together in the middle with string or pipecleaner and use sticky tape to secure. It should make a cross.

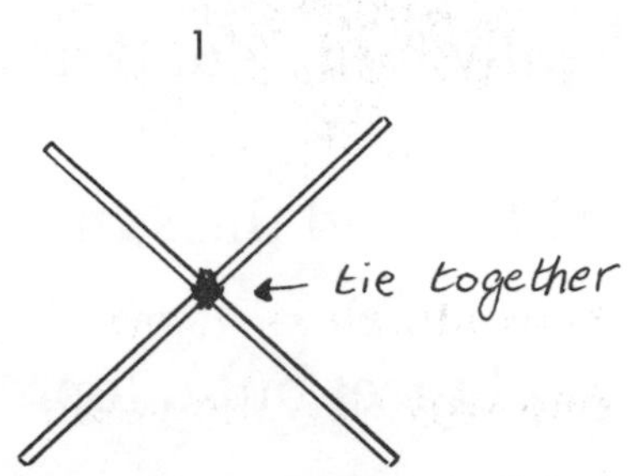

3, 4

2 Tie a long piece of string to the leprechaun's legs and attach to the edges of the two back pieces of wood. Use sellotape to secure.

3 Now tie a long piece of string to the arms and tie to the front edges of the wood.

4 Tie a piece of string from the hat to the centre of the wood.

TO OPERATE: Put your hand in the middle of the wood and move the arms and legs by bouncing the leprechaun up and down.

SING A LEPRECHAUN SONG ...

The Leprechaun Song

As I was walking through Dublin town

I was feeling really happy and not too down,

the sky was blue and the sun it shone –

and who did I meet but a leprechaun!

Leprechaun, Leprechaun, where are you?

Leprechaun, Leprechaun, mend my shoe.

Leprechaun, Leprechaun don't be bold!

Leprechaun, Leprechaun, where's your gold?

You could repeat the song, and replace the town with a different town each time: why not start with your home town?

As I was walking through ________ town,

I was feeling really happy and not too down,

the sky was blue and the sun it shone,

and who did I meet but a leprechaun!

* In verse 2 replace the gap with the name of a town of your choice.

The Irish Famine

About 150 years ago in Ireland people had very tiny farms. But they all grew their own food. That food was the potato – and it was the only food that most people had.

Then a terrible disease attacked the potatoes. When the farmers dug them up from the ground, the potatoes were black and rotten. Nobody could eat them. People were poor and could not buy other food.

A lot of people died. Others went on ships to England, America, Canada and Australia. There are now a lot of people in these countries with Irish connections. Are you one of them?

Irish Music

From the days of the early Celts to the present day music has been very important in Irish life. Lots of people play, from young children to old people. You can see some of them playing on the streets in Irish towns.

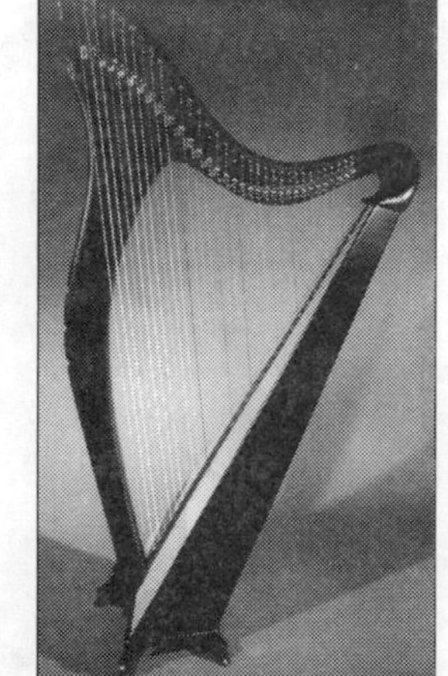

THE HARP

The harp is the official symbol of the Irish nation. It has been used on Irish coins since the year 1526 AD.

THE TIN WHISTLE

The tin whistle is a small, simple wind instrument. A lot of people play it because it is very cheap to buy and fairly easy to play. Nowadays, most children begin to learn Irish music on the tin whistle.

THE UILLEAN PIPES

These are another wind instrument, but they are very different to the tin whistle. They are very difficult to learn.

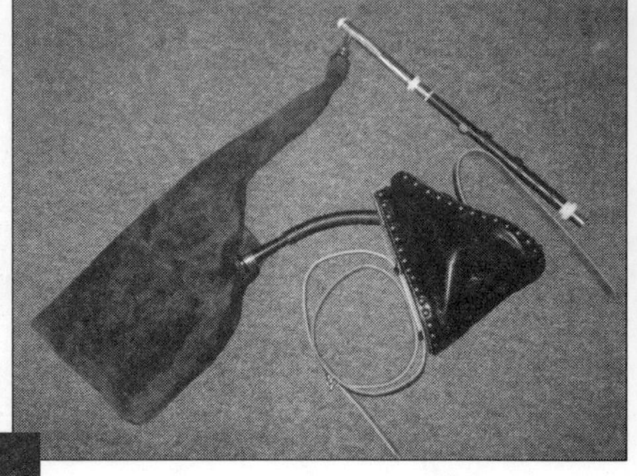

Just look at all those bits and pieces! Some people say it is like trying to play an octopus!

THE BODHRÁN

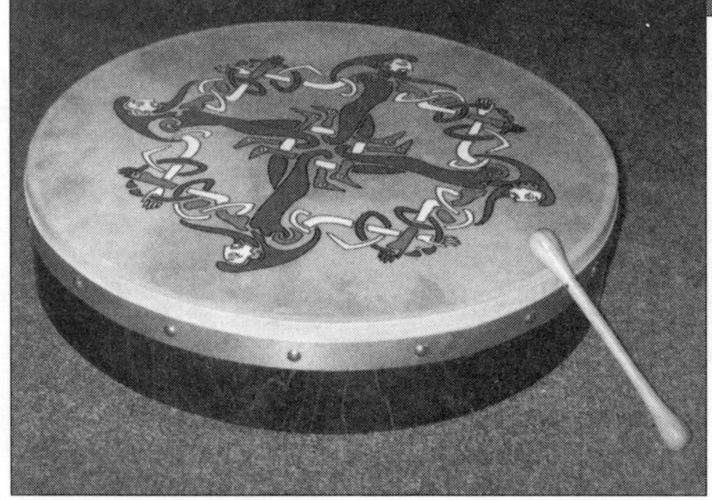

The bodhrán is a small drum which is made by stretching a piece of goatskin over a round frame. It is used very widely in Irish music.

THE FIDDLE

The fiddle is the same as a violin, but traditional music players always call it the 'fiddle'. It has four strings and is played with a bow. It takes a long time to learn how to play the fiddle well. It is the most popular instrument of all for playing Irish music.

Make Your Own Bodhrán

YOU WILL NEED

tracing paper • brown paper and card • thin white paper • black sticky-back felt • paper fasteners • two small sticks • pipecleaner

Cut a long strip of card (enough to go around a dinner plate).

1

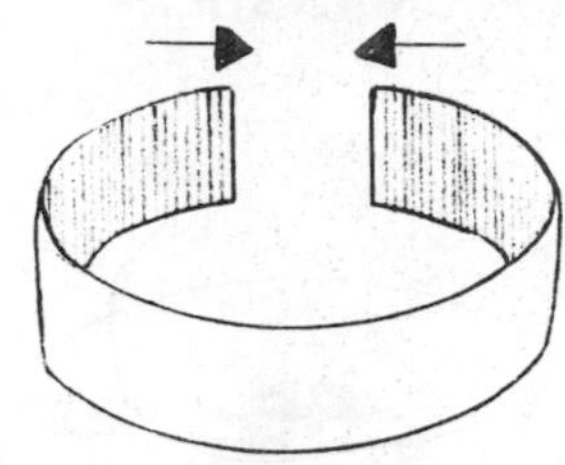

2 Stick one end to the other, making a loop.

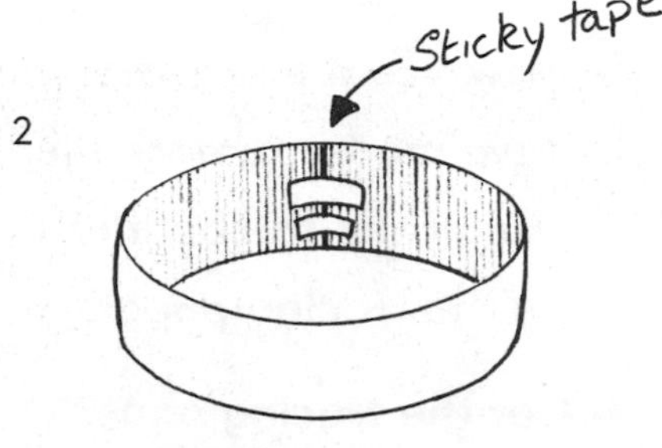

3 Cover this with nice brown paper.

Trace the Celtic design here onto your tracing paper.

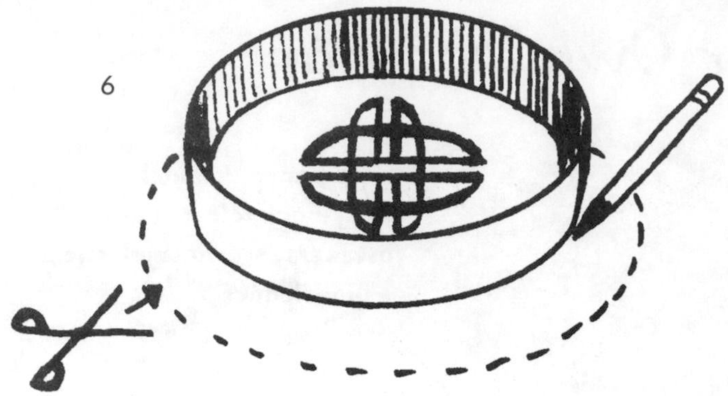

5 Now use the frame you have made to mark the size of the the bodhrán on the tracing paper.

6 Cut the tracing paper outside your mark.

7 Stick this to an equal-sized circle of thin white paper to make the bodhrán stronger.

8

8 Cut in all around from the edge.

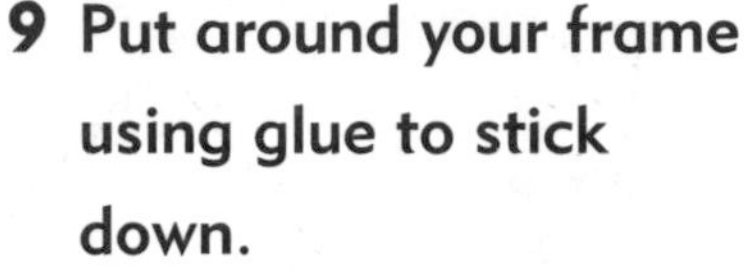

9 Put around your frame using glue to stick down.

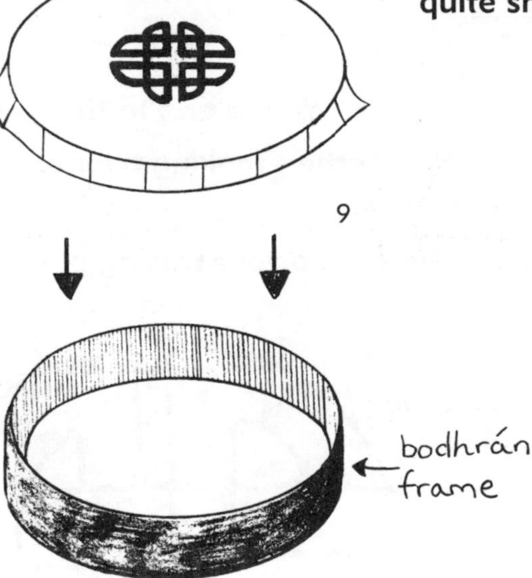

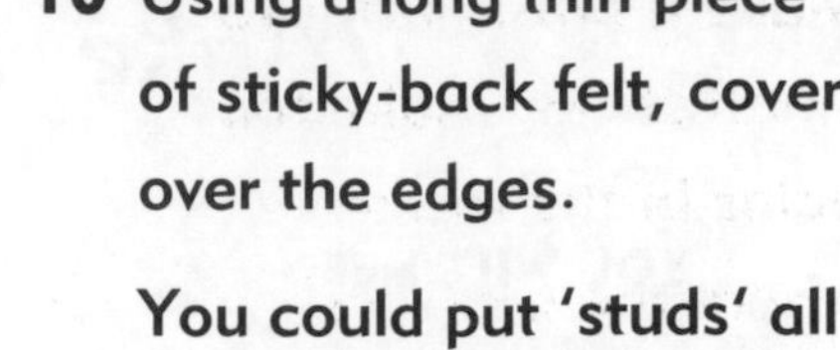

10 Using a long thin piece of sticky-back felt, cover over the edges.

You could put 'studs' all around this by making small holes along the felt and placing a paper fastener in each hole. Make sure you cover them over on the inside with sellotape or brown paper as they can be quite sharp.

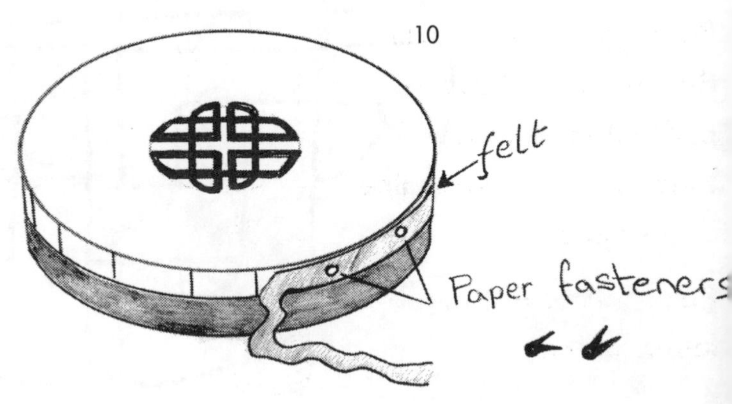

Make a cross with two small sticks. Make four holes in the frame where the cross will meet it. Put the cross into the holes and secure with pipecleaners. This will allow you to hold the bodhrán.

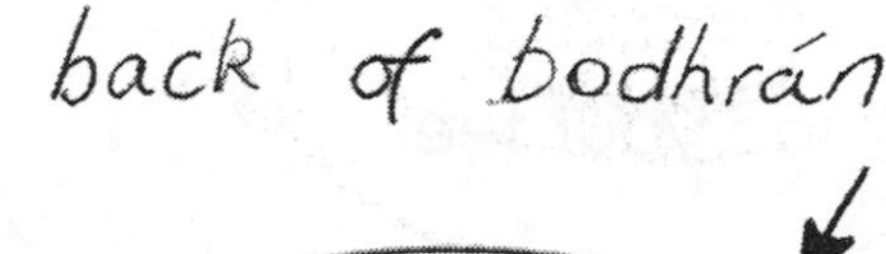

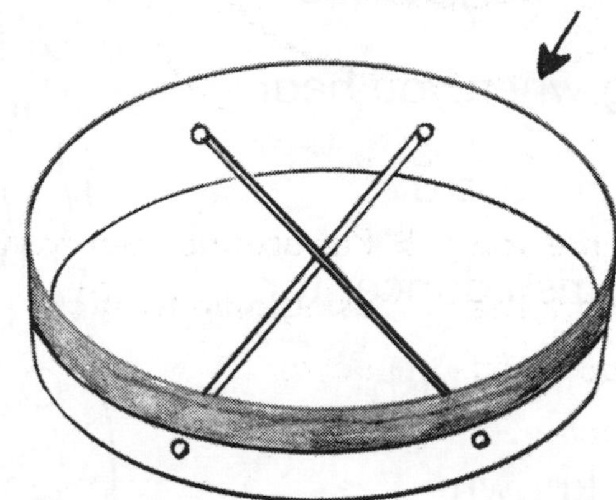

DRUMSTICK

Glue cardboard to both ends of a stick.

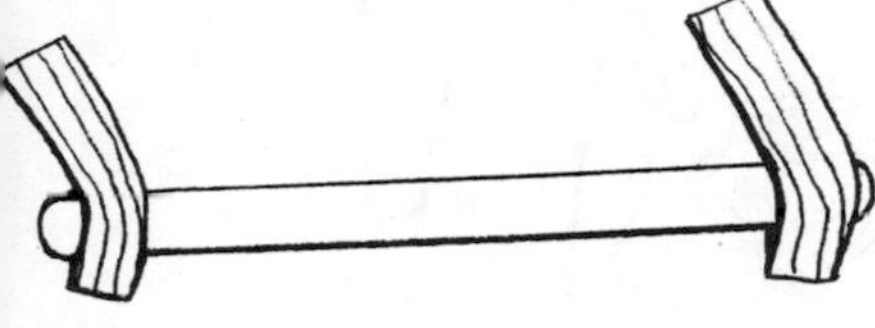

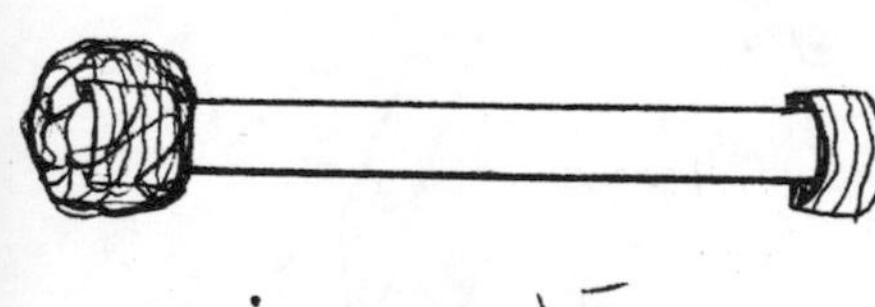

papier maché knob

Put *papier maché* over this to make round ends. Do this three times so you have a nice drum-head.

Paint this brown and leave to dry.

TRADITIONAL IRISH DANCERS

People love dancing to Irish music – do your feet go tapping when you hear it played? Here is a traditional Irish dancer for you to colour in. Irish dancing is known throughout the world. It has very fast footwork but the arms stay very still.

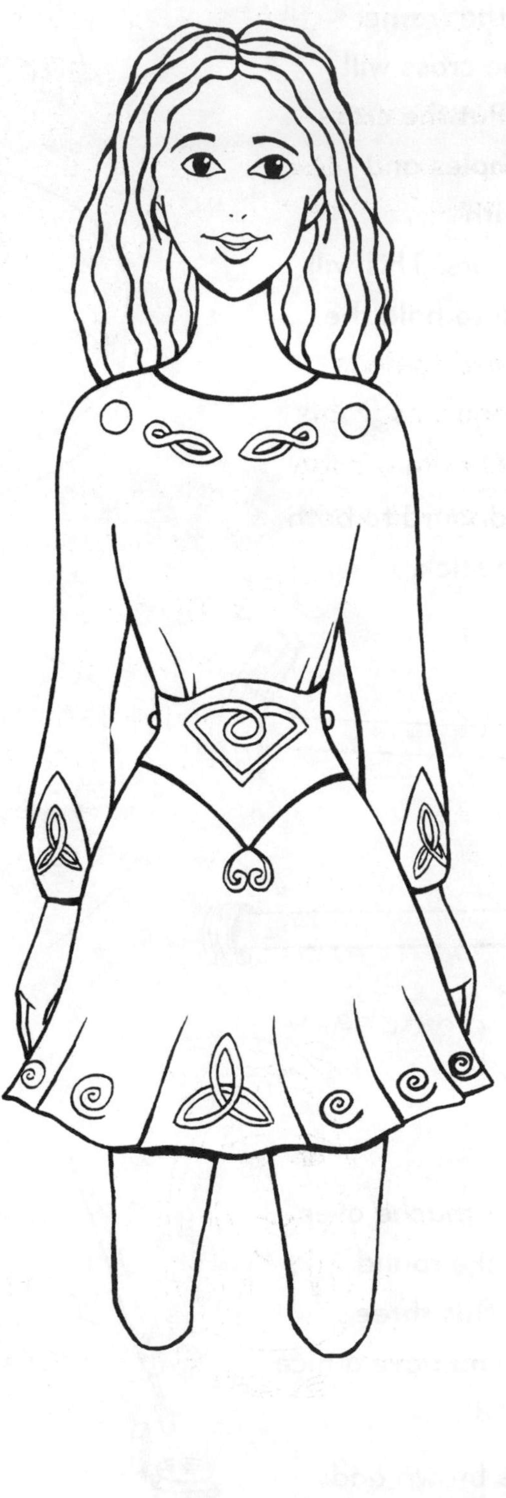

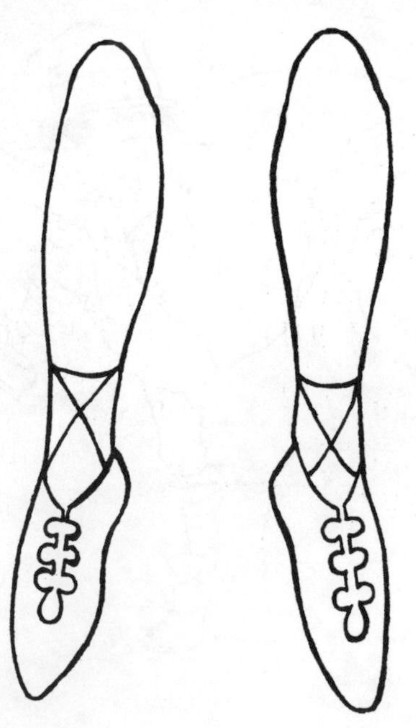

Make Your Own Irish Dancers

Make a colourful dancer – or how about making a row of dancers?

YOU WILL NEED

tracing paper or thin white paper • paper fasteners • thin piece of card • single-hole punch

All you need to do is trace or photocopy lots of dancers onto a page – as many as you want.

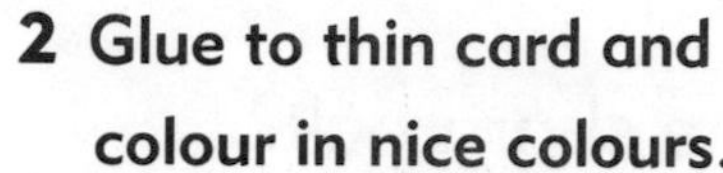

2 Glue to thin card and colour in nice colours.

3 Then, cut out each dancer, and, with a single-hole punch, make a hole through each knee and clip on the leg with a paper fastener. It will move when you bounce it up and down.

4 Now make a hole through each shoulder of each dancer. Put a long, thin stick through the shoulders for your row of Irish dancers.

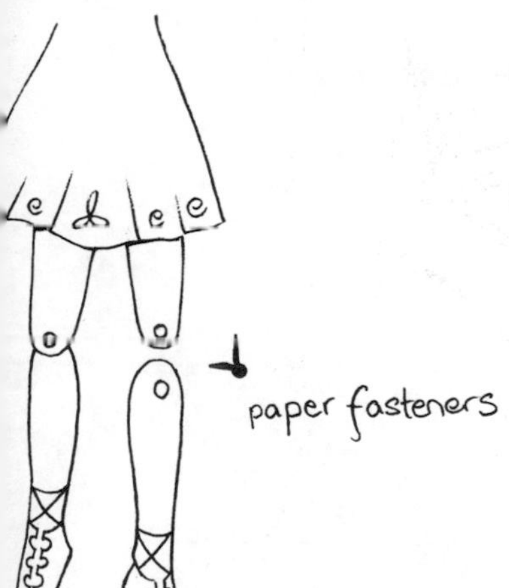

The Shamrock

The shamrock is Ireland's national plant. It is a very traditional symbol of Ireland. We wear a bunch of shamrock on Saint Patrick's day.

Where have you seen the shamrock?

To make your own shamrock badge or fridge magnet – see page 25.

The Irish Flag

The Irish flag is coloured green, white and orange. The green always goes at the flagpole.

The green and orange represent two different religions in Ireland. Most people in Ireland are Catholics, which is represented by the green. The other people are mainly Protestant. This is represented by the orange. The white stripe represents peace between the two religions.

If you would like to make your own Irish flag badge or fridge magnet, go to page 25.

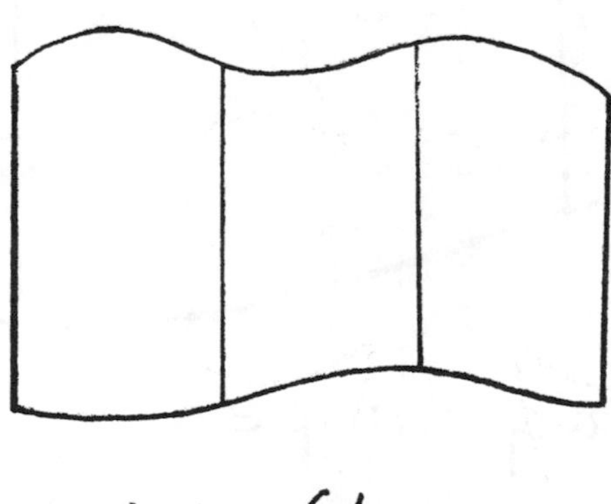

the Irish flag

Make Your Own Irish Flag

YOU WILL NEED

paper • white paint • green and yellow markers • pipecleaners • a small hoop

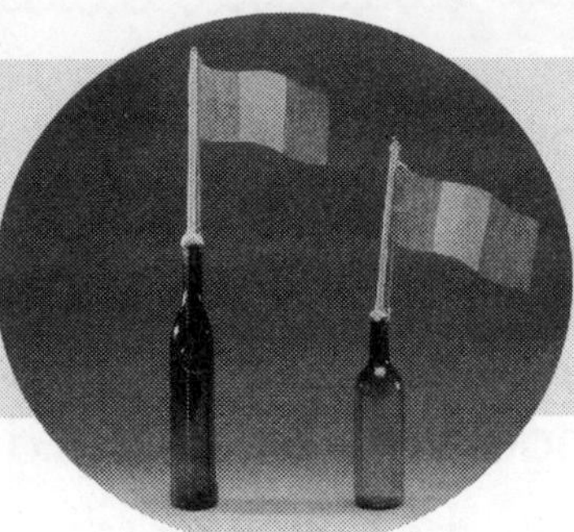

• string • a bamboo stick • a little Polyfilla or playdough • bottle

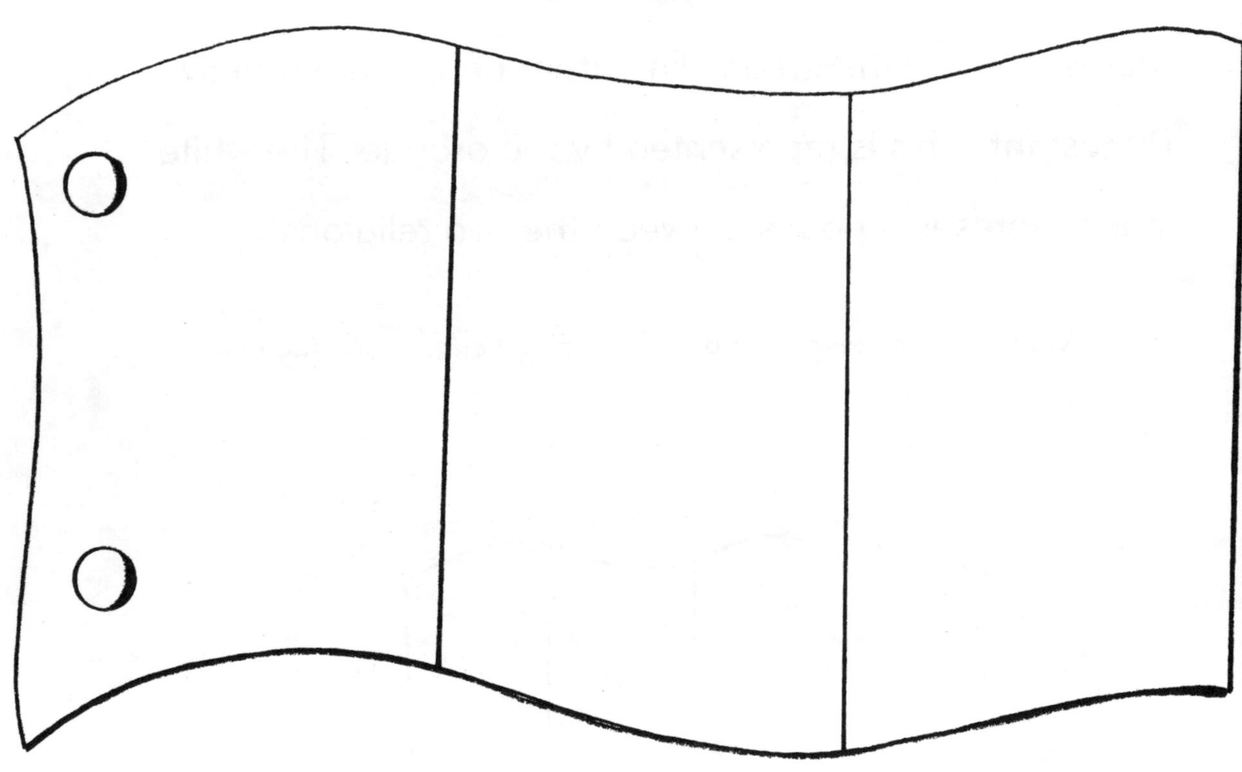

flag shape

1 Draw your flag – try this shape. Colour in your flag in green and orange, leaving white in the middle.

2 Paint a large bamboo stick white, and leave to dry. Then put it in the bottle.

4 small loop

pipecleaner

3 Make a hoop with the pipecleaner. Secure it and the stick with Polyfilla or playdough near the top of the bottle. (If you have used Polyfilla you will need to let it dry.)

4 Glue a small hoop to the top of the bamboo stick.

5 Punch the flag at the top and bottom with a single-hole punch.

6 Put the string through the pipecleaner hoop and the little hoop at the top of the stick. Now put it through the two holes in the flag.

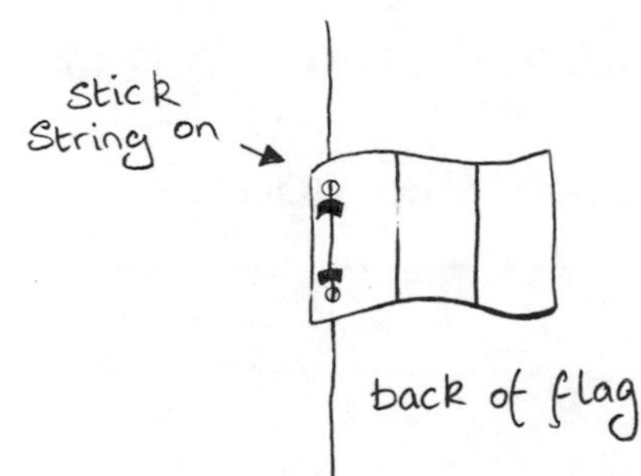

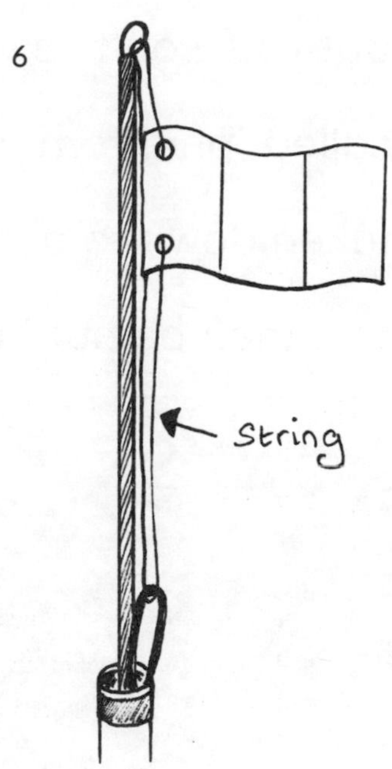

Stick the string to the flag with sellotape.

If you pull the string you can raise and lower your own special Irish flag.

Stone Walls

Ireland is known for its stone walls. These walls are made without using any cement. Holes are left between the stones so that the wind can go through – and the wall won't fall down!

In the west of Ireland there are lots of beautiful stone walls. But you won't see many gates! Many fields have what are called 'phantom gates'. This means that the walls can be taken down to allow farm animals to pass through. They can then be put back together again!

SING A SONG ABOUT STONE WALLS ...

Stone Walls

Stone walls and green fields,
fairytales and spinning wheels,
children playing children's games,
fairies dancing in the rain ...

Chorus

Ireland – a special land of funny ways
and its loveliness shines each day.

Leprechauns in feathered caps,
lovely ladies, friendly chaps,
birds are singing in the trees,
people sing sweet melodies.

Chorus.

1. Stone walls and green fields, fai - ry -
2. Lep - re - chauns in feath - er'd caps, love - ly
tales and spin- ning wheels, child- ren play - ing child- ren's
la - dies, friend - ly chaps, birds are sing - ing in the
Chorus
games, fair - ies danc - ing in the rain.
trees, peo - ple sing sweet me - lo - dies.
Ire -

- land a spec - ial land of fun - ny ways and its

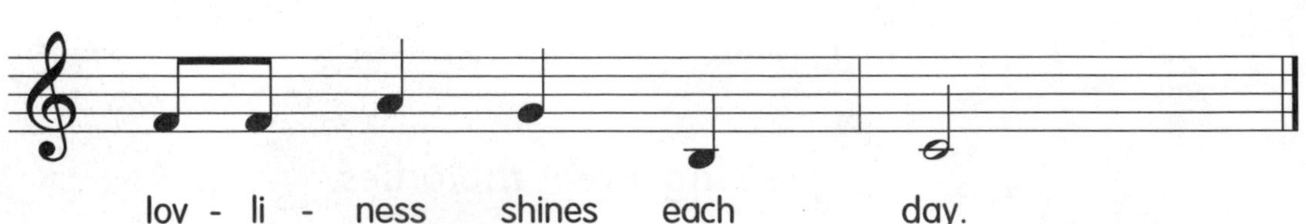
lov - li - ness shines each day.

Irish Money

The first Irish coins have pictures of animals from the Irish countryside on one side. Which animals can you see below? On the other side is the harp. Some coins used nowadays have animals too. Others have Celtic designs.

If you can get a real Irish coin, why not trace it for yourself. Put the coin under a blank piece of paper and use a pencil to make a copy of the coin. All you have to do is go over the paper with the pencil.

You could even trace the front and the back of the coin, cut them out and glue them together.

FRONT

BACK

Now You Can Make Your Own Money Pouch

YOU WILL NEED

paper • plate • felt • scissors • glue

the high cross or other item of your choice from Badge Fun, p.25

THE POUCH

1 Use the plate to draw a circle on a page. Now draw lines dividing the circle into 16 sections.

1

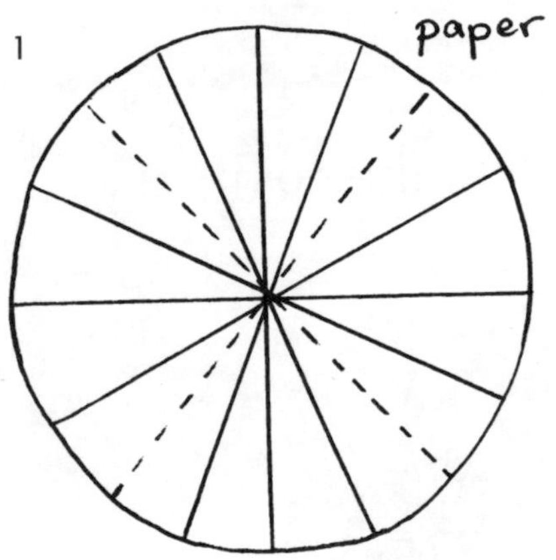

2 Pin the circle to the felt or other material.

3 Cut a hole on each line a little bit in from the edge. Now cut out the circle in the felt.

3

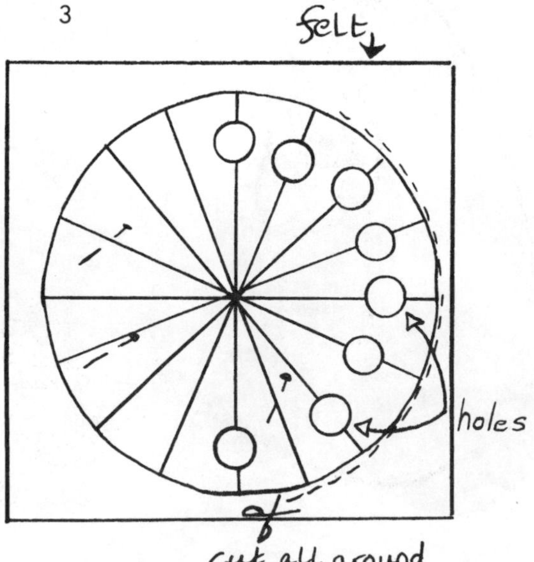

4 Take the paper off and weave the string in and out of every hole in the cloth.

5

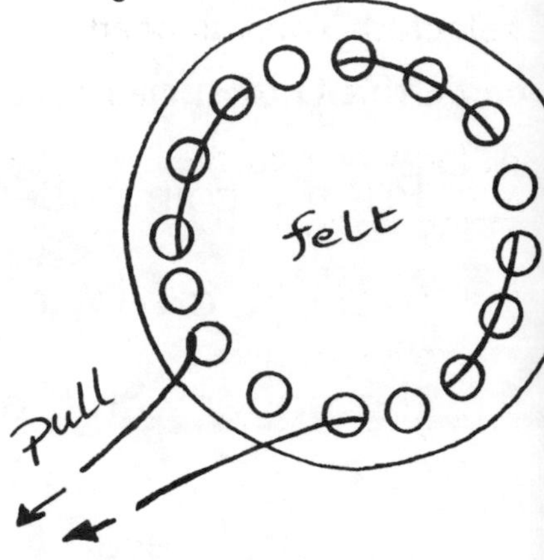

5 Pull the ends of the string. You have made your money pouch.

DECORATION

In the section 'Badge Fun', you made lots of Irish things. Select the one you want for your money pouch – we chose the Celtic cross.

Make two holes in the decoration you have selected. You will need to do this before baking it! Now thread the string through these holes. Tie a knot at the end of both pieces of string to secure!

7

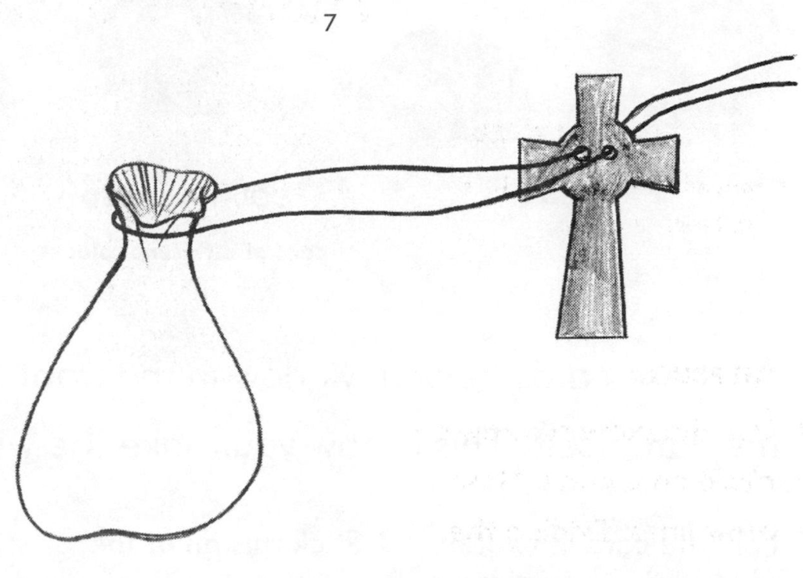

Make Your Own Irish Cards

YOU WILL NEED

- **card of different colours**

All these cards have a window in the front in a different colour to the card itself. This is how you make the window:

1 **Fold the card in two.**

2 **Cut a small square out of the front of your card. Now, cut out a piece of different-coloured paper, bigger than the hole.**

3 **Stick this on at the back.**

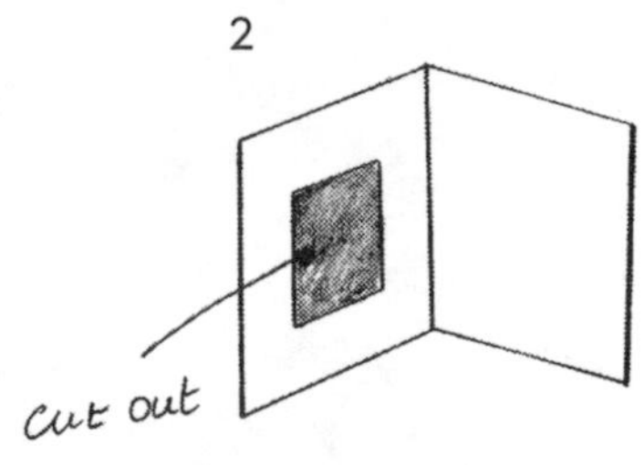

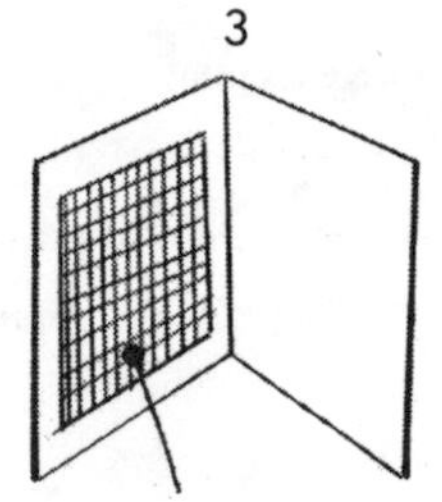

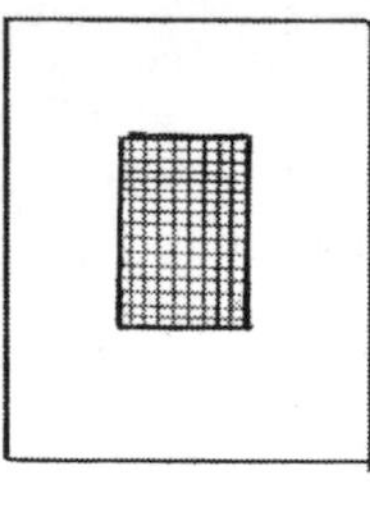

Decorating the Cards

YOU WILL NEED

The things you will need are listed with each card.
Decide which cards you will make then gather your materials.

THE LEPRECHAUN CARD

YOU WILL NEED

a piece of red pipecleaner • white fur • two eyes • green, black, yellow sticky-back felt • fabric glue

Cut the red pipecleaner and fold in two. Stick to the back of the fur.

Stick the eyes onto the card and stick the fur below. You now have the eyes, nose and beard finished!

3 For the hat, cut the green felt to the hat shape. Put a small strip of black felt on it for the hatband, and a yellow box on that for the buckle. Stick these on your card above the eyes.

THE COTTAGE

YOU WILL NEED

yellow fur • white felt • a small piece of brightly coloured felt (for door and windows) • grey pipecleaner

1 Stick a square of white felt on your card.

2 Cut out the door and window shapes from your coloured felt and stick on.

3 Stick on the yellow fur for the roof, and a small piece of white felt for the chimney.

4 Twist the pipecleaner into 'smoke' shape and stick on above the chimney.

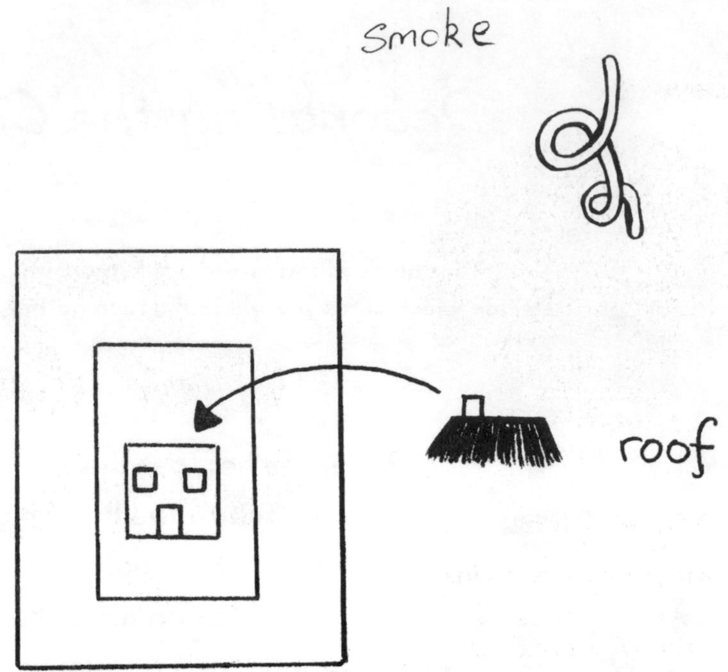

THE SHEEP

YOU WILL NEED

fabric glue • eyes • black felt • white wool

1 Cut the felt into the face shape and leg shapes. Stick onto your card.

2 Glue the eyes onto the face.

3 Twist the wool and glue on the card to make the 'body' of your sheep.

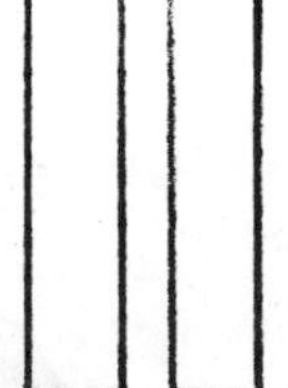

leg shapes

THE SHAMROCK

YOU WILL NEED

a green pipecleaner • glue

Twist the pipecleaner into the shamrock shape and glue onto your card.

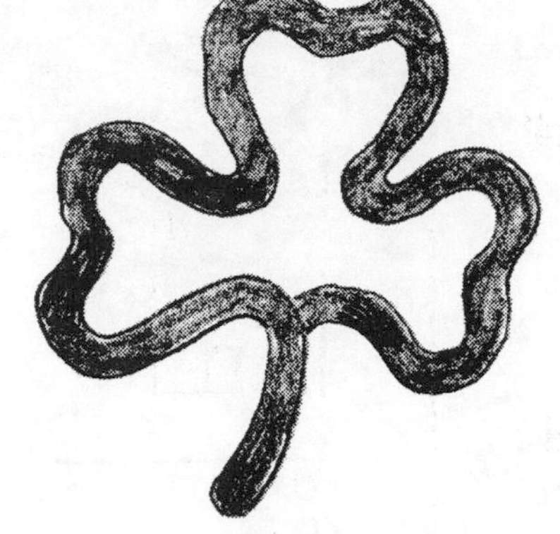

THE BOW-TIE FLAG

YOU WILL NEED

green, white, orange ribbon • glue • black felt for the 'window' • thin string

1 **Fold each ribbon and tie in the centre to make a bow-tie.**

2 **Glue each onto the black felt.**

Make Your Own Bookmarks

YOU WILL NEED

a long thin piece of coloured card for each bookmark • paints • a sponge or old toothbrush • glue •

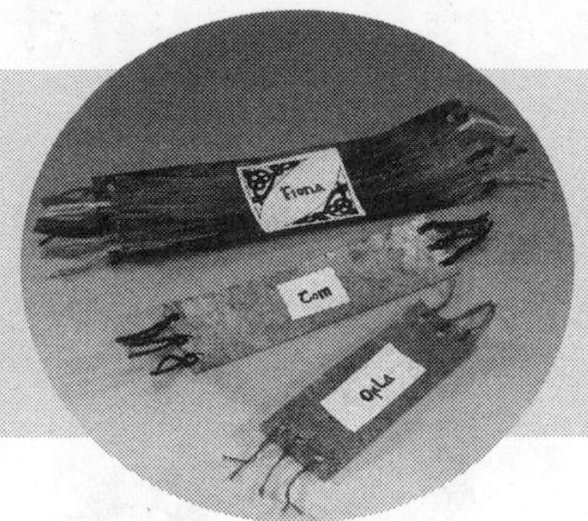

a see-through piece of white paper to trace through • a single-hole punch • colouring markers • wool/string

1 For each bookmark, take a piece of card and punch a few holes at each end with the punch.

2 Use the sponge to print some nice colours on each side of your card.

Or, put paint on the toothbrush and spatter your cards by flicking the toothbrush against a ruler. (Mind the mess!) Allow to dry.

1

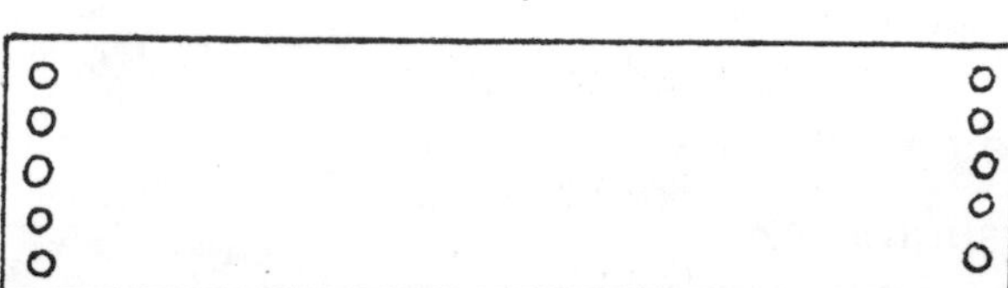

3 Take the see-through paper and trace your name from the Celtic letters on page 28. You could also put some decorations around your name.

4 Cut out around the name and stick this onto the painted card.

5 Cut the wool into pieces, as long as you want.

6 Loop them through the holes, making a knot. Trim them to the length you want.

2

6

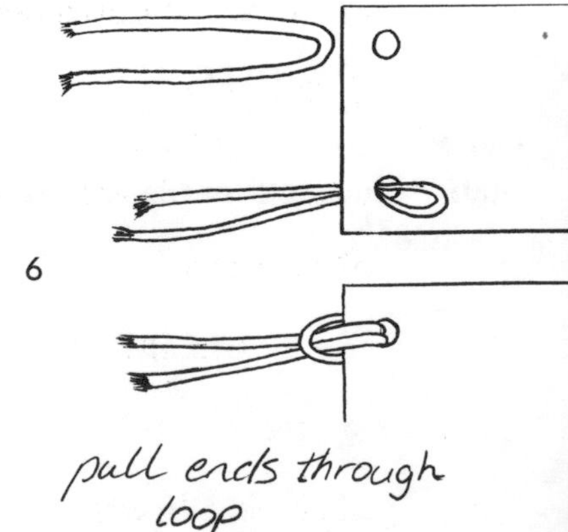

Test Your Knowledge of Ireland

Which of the following is correct:

1 Ireland is an island. This means it is

a) surrounded by water

b) surrounded by trees

c) surrounded by leprechauns

d) surrounded by other countries

2 The patron saint of Ireland is

a) Saint Patrick

b) Saint Brigid

c) Saint Larry

d) Saint Brendan

3 People in Ireland long ago lived in

a) trees

b) tents

c) thatched cottages

d) libraries

4 The special boats used in the West of Ireland are called

a) currachs

b) steamships

c) liners

d) rowing boats

5 Saint Patrick is famous for bringing the following to Ireland

a) leprechauns

b) thorn trees

c) fairies

d) the Christian faith

6 The colours on the Irish flag are

a) pink, yellow, green

b) black, blue, orange

c) green, white, blue

d) green, white, orange

7 The Irish monks were known for making

a) a famous magic potion from apples and apricots

b) chalices of gold and silver

c) trees

d) dresses

8 Which of these are known as the home of the fairies?

a) castles

b) fairy forts and thorn trees

c) people's shoes

d) big houses

9 The leprechaun is thought to be

a) a tiny shoemaker

b) a lemonade drinker

c) a dressmaker

d) a hatmaker

10 Which of these does the leprechaun have at the end of the rainbow?

a) a tin of biscuits

b) an Irish money pouch

c) a pot of gold

d) a pot of glue

9 The famine happened when this became diseased

a) the carrot

b) the potato

c) the parsnip

d) the onion

10 One of these instruments is made from goatskin stretched over a wooden frame

a) the tin whistle

b) the fiddle

c) the bodhrán

d) the harp

Acknowledgements

This project took a long time to create, and due to its diverse nature there are a number of people whom I would like to thank. Firstly, all at O'Brien Press, in particular Íde for her encouragement, patience and expert guidance, and Lynn for her hard work. Also all my family, an anchor of support throughout. The children in America and Ireland who helped with some early creative ideas, especially Myles, Shane, Christopher, Sarah and Emma.

I thank Jimmy McGuinness for photographs and Roger Duignan for photographing the final craft items. Also Clive in Bord Fáilte, Tony in the Heritage Service, Rhona in the National Museum and Shannon Development for supplying photographs for the book. Ivan from Walton's for allowing me to photograph some musical instruments.

Lastly, I thank all of the following people who supported me in many ways throughout and deserve a special mention: Cormac Schollard, Trevor Danker, Billy and Geraldine Parker, Patsy Kavanagh, Anita Murphy, Denise O'Grady, Paul and Orla, Denise Kennedy, Clare Doyle, Noreen Maher, Pat Mahon, and Graham.
Thank you all for your constructive encouragement.

THE PHOTOGRAPHS

The author and publisher thank the following for permission to reproduce photographs:
Bord Fáilte pp.1, 4, 9, 22, 55, 56 (bottom), 66; Shannon Development p.2; Dúchas, The Heritage Service p.30; The National Museum of Ireland pp.31, 32; photographs on p.56 are the author's own.